WORLD OUTREACH

9,500 MILES IN 126 DAYS!

to ALASKA *on a* TRACTOR

Join the 66-year-old Martins on their journey of faith from Dalton, Ohio to Alaska and back on an antique John Deere tractor

GLEN & BETTY MARTIN

For additional copies vist your local bookstore or contact:
Jericho Press
18029 Jericho Road
Dalton, OH 44618
www.milesformissions.org

First printing 1999
Second printing 2000
Third Printing 2003
Fourth Printing 2005

ISBN 0-9677147-0-2

2673 TR 421
Sugarcreek, OH 44681

Carlisle Printing
OF WALNUT CREEK ltd.

Acknowledgments

Many people have encouraged us to share our experiences of this unusual mode of traveling.

We are most grateful to God for peace and protection.

Our sincere thanks goes to Les Troyer for his help in getting this book started. He has contributed several chapters, the foreword, and the conclusion for us.

We appreciate our friend, Deborah Calhoun, who carefully and cheerfully typed up the manuscript.

Glen and Betty Martin

Preface

It is not often that you find people with such a heart to serve the Lord and a burden for souls who have never heard about Jesus.

Glen and Betty Martin have inspired and challenged many to get out of their comfort zones and follow the command of God to go into all the world. Their zeal for missions is matched only by their adventurous spirits and willingness to do whatever it takes to challenge the hearts of God's people to reach the lost in foreign countries.

Hopefully, their testimony of God's leading and provision in this unique mission will stir your heart as you read their journal. Only the Lord Himself knows the eternal results of their willing obedience to set their agendas aside and their hearts on course to journey miles for missions.

Pastor Larry Hasemeyer
Lighthouse Christian Fellowship
1287 Massillon Rd
P.O. Box 31
Millersburg, OH 44654

Foreword

B ooks are the carriers of civilization. Without books, history is silent, literature dumb, sciences crippled. Thought and specula-tion are at a standstill," wrote famous historian Barbara Tuchman. We might add that without the written records of missions, how the Holy Spirit has moved in and through the lives of godly, obedient men and women down across the ages, the building of Christ's kingdom also would be seriously hindered and crippled.

This book is such a record. It is the account of two dedicated people, a man and his wife, who had a vision and did not "neglect the gift within them" (I Timothy 4:14) in their passion to obey the Great Commission as given by Christ in Matthew 28:18-20 for all believers for all time.

Their lack of college degrees or formal, higher education never got in their way when God opened the doors for them to be a witness abroad. With the talents they had, they made an impact for the Gospel wherever they went on their missions trips. This is a book of a simple and yet dynamic faith in action, of people with a devotion that obscured obstacles and ignored critics who might have been tempted to call them religious freaks or fanatics.

Miracles do not seem unbelievable to us when we read of them in the Scriptures, in history, or stories in the past. However, when considering the possibilities of such in real life today, we shrug our shoulders, squirm a bit in our seats, and even hesitate to ponder the possibilities; not so Glen and Betty Martin. In this book you will meet these two hearty souls whose robust faith took them nearly to the ends of the earth—and amazingly, by a green and yellow John Deere putt-putt tractor called "Dandelion"—from Ohio to Alaska and back. That was a miracle in itself!

Read on. As you turn the pages you will be blessed and challenged. And maybe your faith will be stretched and strengthened also to reach out to men and women, boys and girls who have never heard the Gospel, like the Martins have been doing. We hope so!

Les Troyer
Sugarcreek, Ohio

Table of Contents

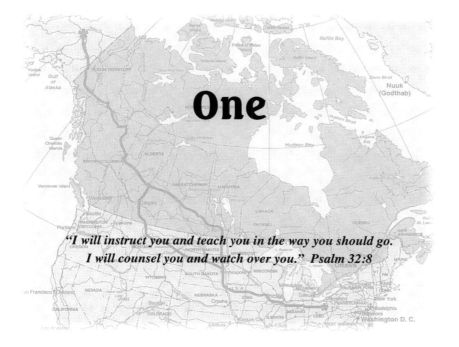

One

"I will instruct you and teach you in the way you should go. I will counsel you and watch over you." Psalm 32:8

T HE HANDS ON THE CLOCK OF THE U.S. Customs Office on the port of entry between the Yukon Territory and Alaska showed 2:00 in the warm, hazy afternoon. The officer's calendar was turned to August 1, 1998. Suppressing a yawn, the man looked out of the office window. Time had dragged on that afternoon. The volume of traffic that last hour had been slow, with only a few vehicles north, in from Canada on the Alaskan Highway.

Suddenly he jumped up from his chair. What he saw in the distance chugging up from the highway toward his station brought a look of amazement and surprise to his weathered face. "Look at that! Over the years I thought I had seen everything on this road, but never a John Deere putt-putt tractor pulling a small Argosy trailer on this highway. I wonder who in the world got such an idea into his head?" He just stood there with his hands on his hips staring out the window in wonder.

My husband and I drove up. Glen pulled back the clutch and then the accelerator on the tractor as we ground to a stop at the customs station entrance and waited in the cab of the bright green and yellow 1950 John Deere Model A. We greeted the customs officer with smiles. Glen stopped the engine so that the noise would not echo under the roof of the entrance. After asking us the routine questions—Where are you from? Where are you going? Are you U.S. citizens? Did you bring any purchases from Canada? etc.—he began visiting with us in friendly fashion.

"Well, I used to drive a model B John Deere when I was a boy on the farm back there in Arkansas a good many years ago. We farmed cotton and used the old John Deere to do all the pulling work. It sure is good seeing and hearing an old putt-putt again!" Waving us on, he wished us a good trip into Alaska as he stood by his small office on the Alaskan Highway watching us chugging away into the distance.

We had finally realized a goal, or at least half of the goal. A dream come true for us—we had driven an antique tractor all the way from Dalton, Ohio, to Alaska for the sake of trying to generate interest in world missions. Of course, we had to drive the tractor back to Dalton again in order to complete our dream. But why to Alaska, of all places? We will tell you later.

Alaska's rambunctious character and independent nature have always been a challenge to many. To some its rugged spirit, its remote, sharp and jagged beauty, inspires sagging spirits. To others, Alaska is almost like a country half finished, half completed. It seems like a country where the extended nocturnal atmosphere stands in the way of its full development. Perhaps the combination of these elements, plus Glen's interest in the state and love for adventures in faith where God has called, provided the impetus for the trip.

For many years the subject of missions has been our passion, and making this trip in such a unique and unorthodox way, we reasoned, would be a means of making people curious who saw us along the way. As we talked with people, we hoped strangers would ask questions and, in the ensuing conversations, we would be able to witness for Christ and encourage funding for Christian world missions. It was a novel idea, to say the least. Last, but not least, we also wanted to encourage other Christians along the way.

Before the Alaskan venture, Glen had made twenty-five short-term missions trips abroad. He had flown to Haiti, China, Indonesia, Nepal, and Tibet on fact-finding missions as well as helping in practical missions-related projects.

The Great Commission of Christ, which He gave just before His ascension, as written in Matthew 28:18-20, has been a spiritually energizing and driving force in our lives. Our adventures on the Alaskan Road were a logical outgrowth of our God-given convictions, vision, and calling, and a faith that gives no room to human obstacles.

Two

by Les Troyer

"Train up a child in the way he should go, and when he is old, he will not depart from it." Proverbs 22:6

G LEN MARTIN WAS BORN INTO the Mennonite family of John J. and Merta (Ziegler) Martin, in Mahoning County in northeastern Ohio. With one brother, John, and two sisters, Ruth and Mabel, who were older than he, Glen enjoyed the status of being the baby of the family. Yet he never was permitted to give in to the natural temptations of being spoiled by affectionate parents and siblings.

His father, a hard-working man, farmed a small grain farm on the rolling countryside and worked in a nearby feed mill. As far back as Glen can remember, his parents and the children faithfully attended the Midway Mennonite Church, which is perched on a knoll in a grove of trees along Highway 46 north of the town of Columbiana, a country town of some 5,000 people. One quickly gets the feeling of being in Mennonite country when seeing the names of Detwiler, Weaver, Witmer, Horst, and, of course, Martin on rural mailboxes along the country roads.

The Midway Mennonite Church is a worn, red brick building with wide cornices. Despite the several apparent additions with newer bricks added over the years onto the original building, the church blends easily into the community. It speaks of growth, of age buttressed with a history of peace and prosperity, of hard-working people, of unpretentious determination, of piety, and of a no-nonsense form of Christianity. It was here in this church and through its ministry that Glen, early in life, accepted Christ as his personal Saviour, which served as a spiritual compass for his life's course.

Farming communities of the area sit anchored by large barns. The tall, round-headed silos silhouetted on the horizon store the silage for hungry cattle. The bulging granaries and carefully groomed farmsteads speak eloquently to the Bible-based values and disciplines of industry, honesty, and integrity of men and women with high moral standards. God has blessed these values that are higher than, and even foreign to, many in the unhappy world around them. Such is the context and the neighborhood in which Glen Martin was born, groomed, and raised.

Betty came into this world near the village of Shanesville, which was later integrated into the larger twin village of Sugarcreek, Ohio. The Hamsher home, a comfortable, white, two-story frame house, sat along Mill Street on the north edge of town, well known for its manufacturing of face brick, as well as being the home of the annual Ohio Swiss Festival. Sugarcreek lies in the picturesque rolling countryside dotted with Mennonite churches and well-kept Amish farmsteads.

The eighth of ten children, Betty also grew up in a Mennonite home known for its deep devotion to the church and to the Holy Scriptures. Milo Hamsher, Betty's father, worked most of his life at the Sugarcreek Farmer's Equity feed mill. Popular with the farmers and highly respected, he eventually rose to become the manager of the mill.

Betty's father, as well as her mother, Ollie (Miller), descended from a long line of Mennonites who were among the original settlers in the communities surrounding Sugarcreek and west into Holmes and Wayne Counties. Both the Hamsher and Miller families were prominent members of the Walnut Creek Mennonite Church and of the village and community of Walnut Creek, which lies west of Sugarcreek along State Route 39.

Like husband Glen, Betty, too, as a young twelve-year-old girl accepted Christ as her Saviour. A godly visiting evangelist, in giving an altar call, included in a simple, ringing call, "When you need new shoes, you don't hesitate to ask your father for new shoes. So why not come now and tell Jesus of your need for Him?" Betty felt the tug of conviction in her young heart and, at the invitation, stood to make it known. Dropping to her knees, she prayed to receive Christ into her life as her personal Saviour. Even at that early age, it was the beginning of a life-changing experience for her; one that she never regretted.

Betty still fondly recalls her growing up years in the bustling Hamsher household with eight brothers and one sister: Dallas, John, Myron, Reuben, Thomas, Mary, Edward, Robert, and James. Life in that household was filled with a vigor that added novelty and challenges to her young life. She also vividly remembers with deep appreciation the evening devotions and prayers, as the family knelt in the living room in their home on North Mill Street. "Then," said Betty, "my dad always ended his prayers by praying 'And when Thou art done with us here below, take us to Thee in Thy better kingdom above. Amen!'"

The twin backgrounds of godly parents, exemplary homes, and strong churches left their impact for life on these two special young people and are evidence of how important the church and family are to the visions and quality of life of our society and the future of our nation.

Three

"Who then is the man that fears the Lord,
He will instruct him in the way chosen for him." Psalm 25:12

O N JULY 4, 1949, GLEN CALLED HIS FRIEND, Ellis Detwiler. The conversation went something like this: "Hi, Ellis? If you're not doing anything special, let's go to Walnut Creek to the Missions Meeting at the church. I hear there are some pretty nice girls down there. What do you say?"

"Sounds good to me," replied Ellis.

"Okay. I'll pick you up in half an hour."

That summer evening was balmy and warm. Filled with the good people from the town and the long, fertile farming valley, the sounds of the hearty singing of hymns in the church wafted out through the open windows of the large, wide, frame meetinghouse as the boys drove into the parking lot. Not only did they hear some good, inspiring preaching and singing, they also met two girls. Glen took me home to Sugarcreek and Ellis dated one of my friends. This was the first time that we met. It was an interesting time of getting acquainted.

Returning again to Columbiana, Glen got absorbed in the daily demands of life on the farm, as young boys did in those days. Then he applied and got accepted to serve on a cattle boat transferring cows to Israel in 1950, part of the recovery plan in the wake of World War II. He made a second trip the following year. Those trips across the Atlantic and to the Holy Land were an eye-opener for him. He got a taste and a sense of what it was like to travel abroad. These experiences helped to condition him for his travels in the days and years ahead.

After his return to Columbiana, he and Ellis tore down and overhauled Ellis' 1941 Chevy and had it working as good as new when they were finished. Glen had a job working part-time in a garage. This enabled him to further hone his skills as a mechanic.

So it was not until about a year later when Glen called me and arranged for another date. Our relationship soon blossomed to where Glen was making steady trips, rain or shine, from Columbiana to the Hamsher home in Sugarcreek. We were in love, and two years later, on November 22, 1952, wedding bells rang as we said "I do" in the same place where we had first met, the Walnut Creek Mennonite Church. We began our married life together in Ohio, settling eventually in a country home north of Mt. Eaton, with a Dalton, Ohio address, where we still live today.

During the late 1940s and early 1950s, the Holy Spirit had been working in both of our hearts. In those years the George R. Brunk evangelistic meetings were making powerful spiritual inroads into the

Amish and Mennonite communities. George Brunk, tall and well-built, was gifted with a robust voice. An expositor of the Scriptures, he came out of Harrisonburg, Virginia like a spiritual whirlwind.

Setting up large tents in the different communities with a well-organized team, Brunk preached the Word of God without compromise, and the Lord used him to bring sweeping revival fires into churches. The revivals were not just some emotional extravagances, but serious movements into the hearts of people across denominational lines. Hundreds were converted and believers' relationships restored with the Lord and with one another.

In some places the nightly meetings lasted as long as six weeks, which was true where we attended, near Orrville, Ohio. Glen was so touched by the deeply searching messages and what seemed like the "sweeping winds of the Spirit" that he drove out to Orrville from Columbiana almost every night. He rededicated his life to the Lord Jesus and His service one evening when Brunk was describing the condition of some believers who had "hearts like stone". Glen did not want his heart to be like that before the Lord.

This experience was special to Glen because of something that had happened when he was six or seven years old. Very early one morning in his bedroom on the farm, he was suddenly awakened as a godly presence filled the room. "It was as though a very bright light shone in my bedroom and the Lord spoke to me. I literally looked around for angels. I didn't see any but I surely felt their presence!" says Glen. He still chokes up with emotion when relating that experience.

Glen knew at the time that it was a supernatural visitation. His rededication at the Brunk meeting related back to that episode and to his deeply felt heart-need for the Lord's will in his life. Today, Glen still traces his call to missions back to that night in the farmhouse followed by the renewal years later at the altar of the Brunk meetings near Orrville. He was sure that the Lord was calling him to something special but did not know what. These were important milestones in Glen's spiritual experience and journey along life's road. Although my calling was not that spectacular, I found Glen's vision and commitments contagious. In time, the Lord honored me with the same convictions and calling as He had given to Glen.

Then there was the time in Kidron, Ohio when Glen was on a business visit in a man's house. As he was finished with the conversation, an Oriental woman staying in the home stepped up and said to Glen, "Young man, I have a word for you. There will be a day when you will go all over the world taking the Gospel with you. You will take the Gospel to kings and queens." Not knowing what she meant, Glen was dumbfounded. Yet he felt that the Holy Spirit was speaking and challenging him through that woman. This all left a deep impression on Glen's heart and mind.

Many years later, after one of Glen's short-term mission trips to Haiti, that woman's strange words returned to Glen's mind again. He and several other Americans had gone to the office of the vice president of the country to ask for a donation of land on which to build some churches. Finally, after clearing with all of the secretaries, they found themselves sitting across the desk from the vice president, and through extended conversations with him, they became friends and he was happy to try to help them with their request.

On Glen's next visit to Haiti, he took along a number of Bibles in French, since that is the basic trade language of the country, and he gave the Bibles as gifts to a number of government officials. Granted, these were hardly "kings and queens"; nevertheless, they were high government officials who often, because of their positions, are insulated from positive Gospel witnesses. This was a deeply moving and inspiring experience for Glen.

Four

*"It has always been my ambition to preach the gospel
where Christ was not known, so that
I would not be building on someone else's foundation.
Rather, it is written, 'Those who were not told about Him will see,
and those who have not heard
will understand.' " Romans 15:20, 21*

GLEN IS NOT SURE WHEN HIS VISION actually began for the unique "Miles for Missions" to Alaska, but he knows that his vision and burden for world missions was drawn into sharp focus one day while looking out over a field of dandelions which had gone to seed. In his testimony to our church, Glen gave the description of the dandelions, which was incorporated into the Internet account of our trip. While he was speaking, an artist drew the picture that is included. Later, in faraway Alberta, Canada, Syd Spiker suggested that we name the tractor "Dandelion." In this book we will sometimes refer to the John Deere by that name.

The Internet information is as follows:

One day as Glen Martin was looking over a field of dandelions that had gone to seed, the Lord revealed to him how the flowers were an example of how He sees the church and His children.

The seeds are like the children of God; although they are individuals, together they form one flower. When they are matured as seeds, the wind, which is like the Holy Spirit, takes them on their journey. Some seeds come off the flower and land very close to home; others drift in a hit or miss pattern across the ground before they stop and take root. Still others fly for miles before they ever reach their destination. God's children leave the security of their lives as they mature in Jesus, sometimes staying close to home and, other times, traveling to the far reaches

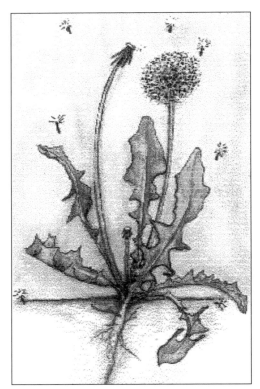

of the world, but always carrying the Word of God forth as they go. A lot of souls can be brought to the saving knowledge of Jesus by one person, just like a lot of plants can come from one flower's seedlings.

The stem of the dandelion is like Jesus is to the church. He is our foundation, the ever-present living God. The stem stays long after the seeds are gone, like a monument to the purpose of each individual seed. When the stem finally dies off and disappears, the root remains, just like Jesus, who died for us, yet who sits now at the right hand of the Father. He remains rooted in our very being and, like the dandelion that has to die before the seeds are released, Jesus died for us and now we can go forth into the world with His word as the wind of the Holy Spirit takes us.

The dandelion is despised by men as a weed: something that is practically impossible to get rid of in the average lawn. This is not unlike Jesus, who was despised by some men and particularly hated by the devil because He covered our sin in His death and that covering is something the devil can never get rid of!

Glen and Betty Martin have a very specific vision of purpose in their lives and that is to reach the lost souls of this world with the good news of Jesus Christ. They have sacrificed a great deal to share this vision with others as they drive their tractor to Alaska and back to Ohio to raise money for missionaries. Won't you please take a moment to pray and ask God if you should contribute to Miles for Missions World Outreach? The need is great and time is short.

Thank you and God bless!

Glen made his first missions trip abroad in the wake of a hurricane that had ripped through Haiti, leaving terrible devastation and loss of lives and property in its path. After eleven years of marriage, coming home from work one evening, Glen heard the news of the storm and the damage. He knew immediately that the Lord wanted him to go to help the people of Haiti.

Two weeks later, he traveled to Haiti where he joined a group of men in construction work. Helping to repair and rebuild ruined buildings and homes, Glen worked hard at the job of witnessing for the Lord. So, in the evenings, after the day's jobs were done, taking an interpreter with him, he gathered children around him and told them Bible stories. Raising the curiosity of adults, Glen was delighted to see many of them beginning to arrive and listen to his stories. He invited them to receive Christ into their hearts and lives as Saviour and some of them did.

On a later trip to Haiti, his group traveled into a very remote place called "Valley of the White". They sent runners out into the mountains telling them that white men were there with good news. Hundreds of people came the next day to hear what that good news was. That day it was Glen's turn to give the message, but he did not know what to preach; so he and his co-workers knelt under a nearby bush and prayed. The Lord laid the passage from Romans 8:11 on Glen's heart as a text: *"And if the Spirit of Him who raised Jesus from the dead is living in you, He who raised Jesus from the dead will also give life to your mortal bodies through His Spirit who lives in you."*

Glen felt the anointing of the Holy Spirit on him as the message flowed freely from his lips out to the crowd. For people accustomed to hearing only bad news, this liberating message of the good news of the Gospel held them spellbound. However, one man in the audience at first did not appreciate what he was hearing from Glen and his interpreter. Staring at them, his eyes filled with hatred, it appeared as though the seed of the Word was falling on stony ground. But when Glen gave the invitation for the crowd to come and stand in front of him to pray for salvation, to their profound amazement, this man was the first to respond.

Glen and his companions were filled with joy to find that the Holy Spirit had taken the Word of God and broken through to this man's very soul. After the service, they learned that the man had been a voodoo priest. How true this passage in Jeremiah 23:29: *"'Is not my Word like as a fire?' saith the Lord, 'and like a hammer which breaketh the rock in pieces?'"*

Since then, Glen has made many other Gospel-related trips to Haiti with Lester Yancey, Aden Yoder, and Sanford Sommers of the "Christian Fellowship Mission," including one trip with Willis Miller from Iowa. On that visit they traveled to a prison island where Glen's mechanical experience stood them in good stead. They had to take a well-drilling rig apart to get it on the boat and then assemble it again after they got ashore so they could drill a much-needed water well. Our son Jim also went along on that mission.

Glen has lifted his eyes to much wider horizons than just Haiti. Since then, he has also traveled to China, Indonesia, Nepal, and Tibet. Longing to help get the Scriptures into China, Glen made seven trips to Hong Kong and many trips into China as a Bible courier. Hiding the Chinese Bibles on his person and luggage, he did get caught a few times by the customs officers, who then confiscated the Bibles. The officials returned the Bibles to Glen when he returned to leave the country, but this did not deter him from continuing on for the sake of the Gospel!

As a young boy, Glen used to be fascinated by Lowell Thomas, the great world traveler and commentator. He never forgot Lowell's descriptions of Tibet. So years later, Glen planned a trip to Lhasa, the capital of that ancient, remote part of the world beyond the high, formidable Himalayan Mountains. Joe Waitkunas, a fellow elder from the Lighthouse Christian Fellowship in Millersburg, accompanied him. Flying from a mission's fact-finding journey to Bali, Indonesia, Glen went to Kathmandu, Nepal, and then on into Lhasa. Glen was deeply moved by what he found.

"I was never so devastated in all of my life by spiritual darkness as I was when I landed in that high, arid country that is caught in the crippling grips of Buddhism," he explains with emotion. "I returned home more determined than ever to pray harder and try to raise funds to do everything I possibly could for world missions!"

I have never been afraid when Glen has left for his missions. The Lord has always given His peace to us as a family, showered us with His wonderful favors, and has taken care of the children and me while Glen was gone. And our four children stood behind our vision as well, never asking why Dad had to go. It was just an accepted fact in our home that their dad's mission trips were something that the Lord wanted him to do, and that their dad was obedient to the Lord's call.

I had several opportunities to travel with Glen to Haiti and China. Once we were also able to take the children along to Haiti. It was a very enjoyable family time. We wanted the children to see what their dad did when he went to the mission fields. It helped to share the vision of world missions.

We recommend that parents take their children to a mission field to observe how the Lord is working in other countries. Exposing our children to such a situation allows the Lord to work in their hearts and minds.

Our friend, Les Troyer, wrote these words: "One can only imagine what a difference such a vision and devotion by the parents could make in the children of the average U.S. Christian family today. It would surely help to reduce the stress and tensions between teenagers and their parents where the world has made its faith-defying, value-destroying inroads into the lives of our young people. Separation from the damaging attitudes, culture, and behavior of the world around them can only work in young people's hearts and minds if there are positive, intelligent substitutes for the vacuums that are left by insisting on such separation."

We have four children and all are married. They and their companions are Mark and Doris Zeck, Dave and Esther Martin, Dan and Carol Martin, and Jim and Jane Martin. There are sixteen precious grandchildren: Deborah and Jonathan (Mark and Doris); Angela and Vanessa (Dave and Esther); Michelle, Ryan, Jeffrey, Melody, Tyler, Kendra, Kimberly, Scott, and Andrew (Dan and Carol); and Matthew, Erin, and Jill (Jim and Jane).

Five

" . . . Pray ye therefore the Lord of the harvest that He would send forth laborers into His harvest." Luke 10:2b

WHEN YOU TALK ABOUT SERVING THE LORD, and begin getting to the crux of it, you'll have to hang on, because you're in for a ride. It is difficult, but it's exciting, too, and the rewards are great!" Glen made this opening comment in a testimony to our church.

Well, we were in for a ride—an estimated 10,000 miles from Ohio to Alaska and back on our Miles for Missions journey. This all began during an eighteen months' time when Glen had been praying earnestly for a way to raise funds to evangelize people in areas of the world where the Gospel had never been heard. His trips abroad to the various mission fields and stations had left him with a heavy weight on his soul, a longing and a burden which he could not dispel. In his mid-sixties, Glen, looking back over the years, did not feel that he had accomplished much for the Lord and for world missions.

One day Glen felt that the Lord was saying, "I want you to raise funds and you already have what you need in order to do it!"

Glen was baffled. What did God mean when He said Glen had what he needed to raise the money? Then as he pondered this, his mind suddenly turned to the John Deere tractor sitting by our shop, which a close friend had unexpectedly given to him.

"But, dear Lord, how can I raise money with that John Deere putt-putt?" he implored.

"Ride it to Alaska and back. Ask for pledges for missions!" the answer seemed to come back.

Glen shook his head. He could hardly believe it at first and struggled with that answer for awhile. Finally, praying for courage, he shared the answer with me. We began praying seriously about this strange idea. I asked "Could we just ride it to Colorado?" No. It had to be Alaska.

Soon after accepting the challenge from the Lord, Glen talked with Marlin Moore, the Millersburg John Deere dealer, and shared his vision. The dealer thought it was a great idea. After all, he and his wife had made a trip to Florida pulling a trailer with their '67 John Deere Model 620 tractor. Why not go to Alaska? "Don't give up your dream!" he encouraged Glen.

During that time Glen was driving for Henry B. Yoder, an Amish businessman from the small village of Charm, Ohio in Holmes County. If we were to make this fund-raising trip to Alaska, he would have to be excused for at least five months from his work. What would Henry say? Would he lose his job? We continued praying.

One day in the spring of 1998, while driving along together on a business trip in New York State, Glen gingerly began sharing with Henry his interest in Alaska and how he felt that the Lord was leading us to sometime undertake such a venture for the sake of world missions. Glen had no idea what Henry's response would be, since he had little background and no experience in world missions.

"When do you plan to go?" asked Mr. Yoder.

"The summer after this one," Glen answered.

Henry did not say much for a while. Then he turned to Glen and said, "Can you take a suggestion from an Amishman? Given the state of world events today and all that is happening, Jesus' return cannot be far off. You should go this summer! And you will have your job waiting for you when you return!"

Glen could hardly believe his ears. He was stunned. Silently he lifted his heart to the Lord, overflowing with thanks and praise. Were the pieces of the plan actually beginning to fall into place? He could hardly wait to get home to share the good news with me.

But then suddenly the reality and enormity of the plan began to hit Glen, as may happen when the Lord begins to answer our prayers—and our dreams. It was already early May. We would have to leave in a few weeks in order to make the trip and be back in the fall before the winter weather set in. The tractor had to be refurbished, a cab had to be built over the seats and controls, plus hundreds of other details that needed careful thinking and accomplishing. The best route to Alaska had to be mapped out for us. And where would we eat and sleep along the way?

The next step, then, meant meeting and discussing this strange venture with our pastor, Larry Hasemeyer. Driving out to his office at the church one afternoon, Glen wondered what the pastor's reaction would be to our plan. Would he discourage us, or say that he would support our idea? But, not too surprisingly, he found in him a ready and enthusiastic faith companion because he too has a burden for missions and believes in the Lord's "soon coming" and that He is still able to do miracles—like watching over two people on a John Deere tractor all the way to Alaska and back!

Moved by Glen's faith and dedication, Pastor Hasemeyer, with little hesitation and growing emotion, said, "Glen, I believe the Lord is in this, and I am going to have a part in it!" (Actually, he figured if God could take Glen Martin on twenty-five missions trips around the old globe, He could take us on an antique tractor to Alaska and back—and it would be a good experience for the congregation to be involved, too!)

The preacher then asked Glen to share the news with the elders of the church. And they almost immediately agreed that they too sensed that the Lord was leading us in this "very different" effort for missions. The next Sunday morning, Pastor Hasemeyer got up to the podium and asked Glen to share his vision with the whole congregation. The people were surprised, amazed, and then excited—in that order. Following Glen's presentation, the pastor recommended that the congregation cover all of the expenses of the venture to help us to get organized and on the road by early June. The pastor and we were delighted when fifteen people stepped forward indicating their wishes to help. One man with computer skills even volunteered to design a web page for the project.

Before that Sunday was over, the church accepted our pastor's challenge and voted to cover all of the expenses of the trip! Volunteers met on Sunday evening and made plans for media coverage and other details. It was obvious that we were "on a roll" and could make plans to leave in early June.

Marlin Moore, the John Deere dealer, heard of the plans being made and graciously offered Glen the use of his twenty-foot Argosy (made by Air-stream) trailer to hitch a ride behind the tractor for the trip. This answered the question of where we would eat, rest, sleep, and keep a record of our daily journey each evening as we traveled along.

The AAA people in Orrville brushed off their maps and helped to plot secondary roads for the Alaskan route because the putt-putt tractor is a slow-moving vehicle. Such vehicles are prohibited on most limited-access highways across the U.S. and Canada. Henry B. Yoder and his three sons designed and built a sturdy metal frame cab with tough plexiglass windows for the tractor and installed two air-ride truck seats side by side in the cab to provide at least that much riding comfort for the exciting journey north.

Since we were not going to need the gripping traction of the treads, Millersburg Tire Service mounted the large, rear tractor tires backwards to reduce the wear and tear on the thick rubber treads. God was already going before us as question after question arose and then was answered in those few, short weeks of preparing for the trip.

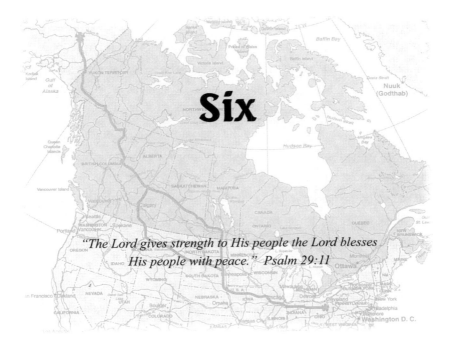

Six

"The Lord gives strength to His people the Lord blesses His people with peace." Psalm 29:11

O N TUESDAY EVENING, JUNE 2, A FAREWELL service was held at our church. It was filled with family and friends. There were words of encouragement, singing by the whole group, and we shared testimonies of gratitude. We were blessed as people gathered around us to lay hands on us as they prayed. What a send-off!

On June 5, all things were ready to actually start the trip that the Lord orchestrated. Only He knew how long it would take. Some family members were on hand to bid Grandpa and Grandma farewell as we climbed up into the cab of the tractor. Glen pressed the starter and the engine sprang to life. He turned out of our drive onto the highway and the journey of faith and adventure northward was begun at 7:30 AM.

Our sister-in-law, Flora Jean Martin, gave us a red silk rose that Glen fastened on the front of the tractor. Enduring all kinds of weather and road conditions, it remained there every mile of the way. Flora Jean also gave us a reminder that said, "Your stops are ordered by God as much as your steps." We put it inside the trailer by the door. Many, many times we could recognize the truth of that statement.

We headed southwest on State Route 241 through Mount Eaton and over the gently rolling hills into Millersburg. John and Flora Jean followed us for ten miles before turning back. As we arrived in Millersburg, some church friends were waiting to pray with us and wave good-bye.

State Route 39 led us west out of Millersburg toward the town of Loudonville. Meeting us there along the road, Andy Millers, Amish friends of ours, talked with us briefly to encourage us on our trip. With all of those good-byes behind us, we were finally on our way, launching out into the wide-open spaces on an adventure of a lifetime, away from friends, family, and people that we knew. The steady throbbing exhaust of the John Deere settled into a comforting rhythm that was to spell out the pattern for the coming days and weeks and months along the Alaskan road.

With a hubodometer mounted on one of the rear tractor axles and calibrated to the size of the tires, we were able to measure the distance of the miles fairly accurately.

The first day we passed through Loudonville and, after many miles on a detour, we arrived in the small hamlet of Wyandot. Dusk had fallen and we realized that our gasoline supply was uncomfortably low, with no service stations in sight in the flat rural countryside. Meeting a man by the name of Virlyn Kenner, we asked where we could find fuel and where we could spend the night.

"I'm sorry. There is no service station close by," he informed us.

With that, we returned to the trailer to discuss and pray over what we were to do on this first night out on the road. Suddenly, Mr. Kenner reappeared: "Hey, I have an extra can of gasoline that will get you to the next station. And why don't you drive on over to the house and park in our driveway? You can hook up to our electricity and stay the night!"

What a providential gift from the Lord, and what a special illustration from Him that He was going to supply all of our needs for the journey! We parked the rig in the driveway and, after a delightful pizza supper provided by the gracious host, we fell into our trailer beds happy for the little trailer and for new friends.

The following morning, we were on the road early, chugging along at thirteen miles an hour. No more detours and, by 5:30 that evening, we crossed the Indiana line on State Route 8, heading for the town of Bluffton.

Indiana ⌒
June 6th

As dusk was approaching in Bluffton, Indiana, Charlie Thompson was relaxing in his house when suddenly he saw the strangest sight passing by on the street out front. "Hey Peg, get your camera and come in here!" he called to his wife.

Peg later said she didn't know if he was seeing a rainbow or what the excitement was all about. He then said it was a deer—a John Deere, that is!

By the time Charlie jumped into the van, backed out of the driveway, and sped on down the highway to catch up with us, we were on the edge of town, wondering where we would park for the night. Since it was Saturday night, we were curious where we would be attending church the next morning.

We were surprised when Mr. Thompson drove up and greeted us. "Come along back with me. You can park by our house and spend the night with us. Our hearts were thankful as we followed Charlie to his home. There we met his wife Peg, who welcomed us and invited us to go along to a restaurant where they had planned to take their grand-daughters, Chelsie and Kendyl. "No one is a stranger in our home!" Peg exclaimed. We concluded that she was absolutely right—they had a friendly brand of generous hospitality.

The next morning we enjoyed going along with the Thompsons to their church, the United Methodist Church of Bluffton. We appreciated the singing and then sharing with the people as the communion elements were served. People were very friendly and curious about our venture. After a meal at the church, we said good-bye to our hosts and headed back out the road again toward Peru, Indiana.

Arriving in Peru, we began looking around for a campsite where we could hook up the electricity for the trailer and spend the night. Stopping at a store to check the telephone book, we were surprised to be greeted by a smiling couple who was out for a walk. After we explained to them our needs they remarked, "We heard about you somewhere. Can't believe we get to see and meet you! Follow us over to our Nazarene Church and you can park there for the night. We will leave the lights on in the church. You can use the restrooms and even take a shower there if you like!"

This was almost too good to be true. We were so blessed to be invited and it did not take us long to accept that providential hospitality. The next morning we accepted the invitation of Pastor Tony and Margaret Winter to breakfast and a happy time of fellowship together in the Lord.

On the way west through Burnettsville, while stopping to get gas and to pick up some lunch, a newspaperman came up to us, wanting an interview. He had heard the chug-chugging of Dandelion and ran over to see what was happening. Along the top edge of the cab, the words "Miles for Missions" were painted in green on a yellow stripe. A white banner was strung across the back of the trailer with the words "Miles for Missions World Outreach" and "Ohio to Alaska and Back". People naturally stopped out of curiosity to see what this was all about.

We had an interesting diversion while traveling through the village of Reynolds. To our surprise, the sheriff stopped us. "I wonder what on earth he wants!" Glen said to me. "Surely we weren't speeding!"

The sheriff, although business-like, requested in a friendly manner that when we see more than four vehicles lined up behind us, since we traveled only thirteen miles an hour, that Glen should pull over and let them pass. Then the officer smiled and said, "I hope you get to Alaska okay."

Illinois ∿
June 8th

By 3:40 we got to the "Welcome to Illinois" sign. We had driven through lots of "liquid sunshine". Since Glen had a slight cold, we decided to stop earlier that evening. Stopping at a convenience store at the edge of town, we inquired if anyone knew of a pastor and church we could contact to park our rig. A man with three packs of cigarettes in his hand said, "There's a church just down the street whose pastor is Jim Harkins." We drove across the street to Motel 8 to call Pastor Harkins. This friendly man met us at the motel in a few minutes. In answer to our request to park at his church, he replied, "I would rather have you stay here at the motel and our church will pay the bill." He gave us a pleasant smile and hearty handshake, talked to the receptionist and left. It was evident that Glen needed rest when he went to bed at 8:15.

In the morning we went to the lobby for the continental breakfast. The manager, Brian Short, was there. It was interesting to get acquainted with him. He suggested we stay another day and night because the weather was rainy and windy and just plain miserable. "I'll pick up the tab," he said. We found it difficult to resist his kind offer. Staying dry and getting more rest proved beneficial.

From there we putt-putted on west and then northward on Route 47 toward the town of Plano, lying southwest of Chicago. An hour before arriving in town, we called longtime friends John and Roberta Ressler. Living in Sandwich, only about five miles west of Plano, the Resslers were delighted to meet us along Highway 47 for a short and happy visit in a Burger King.

As the miles churned along and away under us, we met other friendly, curious, and helpful people in Illinois. We met Reverend Jim and Ruth Freund of Genoa, as well as Rich and Carol Frey in Mt. Carroll, who called a news reporter to interview us. This gave us publicity for our missions endeavor. Reverend Freund had a great sense of humor. He told us that plans were being made to build a town between Sandwich and Plano. They planned to name the town Bologna. The area would then be a "Plano Balogna Sandwich". (Whew!)

Iowa ∿

June 11th

On June 11th, we crossed the mighty Mississippi River and putt-putted into Iowa. From the flat prairie lands of Illinois we were now coming into a series of low, rolling hills and lots of flooding because of recent rains. Along one stretch of road a long line of vehicles was waiting because of roadwork.

A flagger girl came up to the tractor to see who we were and the purpose of our strange-looking rig. Glen gave her several of the "Miles for Missions" brochures and she asked him, "Are you of the 'born again' belief or the 'new way'? I am seeking the truth. But I don't know the meaning of either of those terms!"

Glen explained to her that the Word of God is the truth and is given in the brochure. She was very grateful for them. I saw her giving brochures to the other flagger girls that were working on the road. This was encouraging and we welcomed the opportunity to sow the seed of the Word into the minds and hearts of people like her along the way.

Iowa is a wide, sprawling state with acres and acres of beautiful farmland and good roads. We were making good time, often averaging over a hundred miles in a day. When we arrived in Oelwein, we began seeking information on where we could spend the night. We laid our hands on the map and prayed, asking the Lord to lead us.

Two men were working nearby, but didn't know of a place that would accommodate us. "Hey, I'll bet Joe might know," one of them said. "He's in that white building over there."

So we walked over and met Joe. We asked him where a good place would be to park for the night. "Come into my office," he said. "We'll try to arrange something." We could tell that the "wheels in his head" were turning. Then he called his wife.

After a short chat on the phone, during which he told her he was bringing company home, he said, "Follow me over to our pond. We have a perfect place for you to park!"

And, as he had said, it was a perfect place to park the John Deere and the trailer. Joe and his wife Barbara were really congenial hosts. Joe contacted the local John Deere dealer in town and had him check the tractor carefully to make sure that it was in good condition to continue on across the state. He was instrumental in having our "story" published in the Waterloo Courier since our tractor was made in Waterloo, Iowa.

So far along the journey, we had had a variety of responses from motorists on the road. One semi truck driver pulled off the road in front of us. Not knowing his reason for doing so, Glen thought he might be angry for our having slowed him down with his big, husky truck. But he came back carrying a strobe light. "Here, you might need this along the way," he said with a smile. (We had a strobe light unit on top of the trailer to warn oncoming traffic of our slow-moving vehicles.)

Many passers-by waved at us to show approval. Others craned their necks and stared. Out of the town of Oelwein, a highway patrolman passed slowly and waved with a friendly smile. It was encouraging to see how many people seemed to approve of our "Miles for Missions" venture.

In the Hampton area, where we needed to buy gas, a man came walking toward us. We immediately knew he was a farmer. It turned out Dale Mollenbeck was like a tour guide. He had us park the tractor and then took us all over the town and country to find a place to camp.

He then took us along to the Zion Reformed Church the next morning. As an added bonus, Dale and his wife Norma took us along to a family reunion, quite a contrast and break away from riding that antique John Deere putt-putt all day! Later that day, we parked the rig at the home of Dale's brother Delmar and sister-in-law Ellen in Hampton for another good night's rest.

Further on down the road the next day, on the way to the town of Cherokee, we stopped at a truck stop for coffee. To Glen's surprise and amazement, he was paged to come to a telephone. A reporter from a local radio station wanted to interview Glen. How that happened is a mystery to us.

When traveling that distance, one can assume a person would make a wrong turn at least once in a while, and that is what happened to us. Leaving the small town of Clarion, we drove south for a good hour instead of continuing west before discovering our mistake. Correcting our route back was a challenge, especially since we had to do it in heavy rainfall. But the journey was sweetened by knowing where we were to sleep that night.

A couple in the church the previous Sunday had encouraged us to stay with their daughter and family in the Cherokee area. Despite our arriving late, Ivan and Darlene Wiersema had a delicious hot meal waiting for us. What a reassuring feeling it was to meet so many fine, dedicated, warm-hearted Christians along the way!

Along the route the next day toward South Dakota, a pickup truck with four people in it flagged us to stop. These four people were all excited about the concept of "Miles for Missions" and promised to call the local TV station to come out and do an interview, but none showed up. A little later another pickup truck came along with three guys in the cab. One of them dangled a five-dollar bill from the window and signaled Glen to stop. We were disappointed that the fellows were not interested in missions. They just wanted to see the tractor! Why the caper with the five-dollar bill, we will never know, but it was added to the mission fund.

South Dakota ~
June 16

On June 16 at 3:30 in the afternoon, we arrived in South Dakota. Now we had been on the road for eleven days. It was warm and we needed a change of pace, relief from the steady grinding of the tractor gears and the throbbing of the exhaust stack. Arriving in Beresford, South Dakota, we checked in at the local Crossroads Motel and, to our pleasant surprise, found that the owners were dedicated Christians.

I was courageous enough to ask the owner of the motel if I could do one load of laundry. She kindly consented. My journal reminds me that it was quite warm and the air-conditioning felt so good. The last sentence for that day was, "We will try not to get spoiled."

The next morning, with lightning flashing on the northwestern horizon and dark, threatening storm clouds gathering, we wondered if we should start out on the road again. The weatherman on the TV weather channel gave warnings of the approaching storms. Common sense dictated and we checked in to stay another night. Glen decided it would provide opportunity for him to caulk seams that were leaking along the tractor cab. But he did not know how he would reach the top, since he did not have a ladder.

While he was standing by the tractor pondering what he should do, a seventy-six-year-old farmer came along and engaged in conversation. Glen told of the need for caulking. "Hey, I'll take you to a hardware store in town to buy the caulking that you need. Come on, jump into my car," he said.

Returning again to the motel, our "Good Samaritan", who said he knew everyone in town, went to the motel owner, borrowed a ladder, carried it to the tractor, and held it steady while Glen did the caulking job. How thankful we were the next time we traveled in the rain—no more dripping raindrops on us. It may seem to have been a small matter to others, but to us it was again proof that the Lord was watching over us and meeting our every need!

On up through South Dakota we traveled, steadily northward on Route 281 through towns like Wagner, Corsica, and on up to Aberdeen. In Wagner a reporter came by to talk with us while we were having the front tires on the tractor switched at a John Deere dealer's shop because one side was wearing faster than the other. At the shop, an old John Deere tractor buff said to Glen, "Your tractor could go to Alaska six or seven times. They're tough tractors!" Glen had to laugh at the old-timer's enthusiasm.

In Corsica, Don and Henrietta Star kindly offered us parking space, shower, and restroom accommodations in their home because their Parkway Motel was filled. They were just one in so many fine, generous people who God provided for us as evidence of His loving care on our journey.

Route 281 is straight as a rail and extends on through Aberdeen up to the North Dakota line. In the flat lands, especially in the prairie country with few towns, driving gets boring and a feeling of loneliness swept over me. We could make good time on this lonely road. We drove miles and miles past thousands of acres of farmland at times without seeing any farm buildings, not much traffic, and very few towns. Speaking of signs along lonely Route 281, there are only two signs: "No Passing" and "Adopt a Highway". But who would want to adopt a highway out there at the end of nowhere? We traveled for hours of peaceful putt-putting. I say peaceful because there were not many vehicles on this stretch of highway. I sang many songs, but Glen could not hear me. He had his earplugs in!

Around noon on June 20, we arrived at the home of Glen's cousin James Ziegler and his wife Kathlyn, who live on a farm west of Aberdeen. What a happy reunion this was! After catching up on all the news, I did some laundry while Glen did maintenance work on Dandelion, the tractor. He had a telephone interview with a reporter from the *Aberdeen American Morning Star* newspaper. This also gave the opportunity for us to call back to Ohio to our families to assure them that all was going well on the trip.

After attending church with the Zieglers (which included Dale, another cousin) on Sunday, we left bright and early on Monday morning, grateful for the short but pleasant interlude we had with our friendly and hospitable cousins. North of Aberdeen, a car swerved past us and stopped. Out jumped two John Deere tractor enthusiasts all excited about the antique tractor. Quickly taking photos, Kenny Ham and Bud Dennert then called friends five miles up the road who later were out by the highway to see us and the tractor as we drove up.

North Dakota ∼

June 22

_____

At 12:40 PM on June 22 the sign "Welcome to North Dakota" appeared along the way. Moving along at our steady thirteen miles an hour, we were surprised to be stopped again by a state trooper. "One of your flashing lights isn't on," he remarked. (Small oversight, but necessary for slow-moving rigs.) The patrolman then asked about our mission and Glen described what our aim was for the journey.

"That sounds great," the officer replied. "More people should be doing things like that for God."

Glen then asked him if he was a believer and he said, "Oh yes, I am born again. I accepted Jesus as my Saviour back in the 1980s. Then he shared a prayer request for people to whom he had been witnessing about salvation. Accepting a number of our brochures, he thanked us and left again, apparently happy for the opportunity to have fellowship with Christians along the way. This was a special part of our day. He gave us his card and said we should call him if we have any kind of problem in North Dakota.

On Tuesday, June 23, I wrote in my journal: "Today we faced the second detour of our trip. It took us four hours to cover 33 miles from Jamestown. And I must say, it was the loneliest stretch of road we've been on so far. The few families who live along that road must be courageous. I admire them for their ability to hang in there! It rained all the way!"

The route continued straight as an arrow up through North Dakota, with little relief from the monotony of the endless, sweeping landscape; of broad, distant horizons and the wide, overarching canopy of prairie skies. Still, the little antique John Deere Model A moved faithfully along—mile after prairie mile—toward our destination.

We found the people in the town of Jamestown to be friendly and we parked at the Frontier Camping site where thirty people came with cameras clicking. Glen checked and we had clocked up 1,556 miles so far on our venture. We stopped at the local John Deere dealership to buy a steering knob and mirror. There was a lot of interest in our rig generated at this dealership.

The following night we camped in a Kiwanis campground in Carrington, recommended by Ray Azure. Ray is a barber and also a "Good Samaritan" type of person. He brought us cheeseburgers, fries, and coffee after calling Dwayne and Donna Weber, who came to join us for conversation at a nearby picnic table.

The next day the rain and lightning continued, making travel less than pleasant. Route 281 was under construction and renovation in stretches. This slowed the tractor down. Because of all the rain, floodwaters were spreading everywhere. We were told that only five years earlier, Devil's Lake had been located nine miles to the east of the road, now the lake had reached the road because of the heavy rainfall. Construction crews had raised the roadbed to protect it from water erosion.

We met Dave Leas at Rocklake in the only restaurant in the village. He explained that it was a very depressed farming community. "People have been moving out so fast that only around 50 families remain in the area. It won't be many years until everything in town will be boarded up," he said. When he was a senior, they had over 120 students in high school. Now there were only 90 left in kindergarten through 12th grades!

Through his gracious courtesies, Glen was able to park the rig by the United Methodist Church where we could hook up the electricity and use the restrooms. The next day, when we were ready to leave, the tractor starter refused to crank. Pete, a local mechanic, came running to our rescue. They found a bad cable connection to the battery. In a short time we were on the road again.

Seven

*"The man who plants and the man who waters have one purpose,
and each will be rewarded
according to his own labor." 1 Corinthians 3:8*

Manitoba ∽

June 25th

O N JUNE 25, WE FINALLY ARRIVED at the Canadian border in the province of Manitoba at the International Peace Garden entrance. Being ushered through customs was relatively easy.

"Are you American citizens?"

"Yes."

"Do you have any alcoholic drinks or firearms in your possessions?"

"No."

"How long do you plan to stay in Canada?"

"As long as it takes to get to Alaska!" Glen answered with a smile.

She waved us through.

Pulling into the lane at the customs booth, Glen had to drive through a patch of tar. What a mess! Pieces of tar-covered gravel from the tires flew everywhere, up into the cab and over my clothes and purse. Up the road a stretch, we stopped, got paper towels out of the trailer, dipped them into the gas tank, and cleaned up as best we could. After this mishap we traveled until evening on Canadian Route 10.

In the town of Souris, we stopped at a tire business and had them reverse the front tires on the rims so they could wear evenly on the other side. When Glen got his billfold out to pay, the owner said, "No charge. That can be my contribution to the cause."

We slept in a place called Victoria Park in the Souris area. This park had the nicest facilities of any so far along the journey north. When the park manager learned the purpose of our trip, he waived the parking fees.

We went through the routine of fastening our seat belts and pushing in our earplugs. The tractor was humming its usual "tune" and then it started to rain almost like a cloudburst. Since the bottom side on the front of the cab was not rainproof, we had to pull large (30#) black plastic garbage bags over our legs and laps. This proved to be an inexpensive way to stay dry. Driving on through the rain, we came to the small town of Hamoita, where the rain finally stopped. We got a bite to eat there. People came running up, as usual, to ask questions. Again, as always, we had an excellent opportunity to witness to them about the Gospel and the vision we had for the journey.

We had a destination in mind—Shoal Lake—where we wanted to spend the night. We got there early enough to park and go for a walk by the lake and through part of the town. This exercise was essential for us. There were very few campers but many mosquitoes. Glen found a tick on his arm that was just beginning to dig its way down to suck blood. I made sure the tick didn't achieve its goal.

In Shoal Lake, we stopped for gas at a full serve station. The woman attendant looked at the tractor in a perplexed way and asked where to fill the tank. She was full of fun and chatter. Needing to check the tractor, we drove to a John Deere dealer's place where they examined the grease seal and the bearings in the rear wheels. They also replaced the strobe light on top of the trailer that had stopped working. This did not take long and we were on our way again. As we left for Russell, Manitoba, the sun began to shine. What a relief and an enjoyable change that was for us!

After pulling into a station for gasoline, we noticed three men sitting in a truck looking at the front end of the tractor. Asking about the trip, they called Glen's attention to the small front tires where the rubber had worn through, in some places exposing the cord. "There is a tire shop just a block from here that probably carries tires that size," the men said.

At first the dealer thought they didn't have the size needed. What would we do if they did not? Glen felt very sure they had the tires. Now if only we could convince the workers. After checking their inventory again, the dealer found the right tires and mounted them on the tractor. That was a definite appointment of God to have those men talk with us and we rejoiced as we got back on Route 16 and were spared from having had a blowout. Daily we had special evidences of God's protecting care as we moved along north.

Saskatchewan ∾ ————————————————————

June 27th

During the next portion of traveling we hit heavy rain showers again and at 5:55 in the evening we saw the sign "Saskatchewan Naturally". Stopping at an attractive information center on the outskirts of the town of Lagenburg, we inquired about churches in the town and chose a church pastored by Reverend Jack McNeil, who immediately invited us to park by the church. We were welcomed to hook up to an electrical outlet for the trailer and to use the facilities. He and his wife Leona and their daughters then took the tractor team out to a pizza place for supper. The next morning we worshiped with the McNeils in their friendly church. We felt right at home with the hymns and praise songs they sang and the message by the pastor from Acts, the 20th chapter. After the service, Tony and Pat Petracek treated us to Sunday dinner at a nearby restaurant. That evening Glen spoke in their service. It had been an inspiring and eventful day—another one blessed of the Lord.

After making several telephone calls to the family back home in Ohio, we were out on the road again at 7:30 in the morning, heading north and west toward the province of Alberta, putt-putting along at the usual thirteen miles an hour. That evening we stopped in at the Gospel Fellowship Church in Foam Lake, where Reverend Dennis Thiessen serves as pastor. He called several older fellows who he knew were also John Deere tractor buffs. They came to the church to see us and, of course, the plucky little antique John Deere putt-putt. We learned that these men had left Russia with their parents to escape communism when still small children and grew up in Canada.

While browsing at the information bulletin board in Pastor Thiessen's church, to our surprise we saw notice of an upcoming concert by singers "Grant and Sally" at the United Church in town on July 5. Grant and Sally are from our home church! What a small world, indeed! We then met the pastor and his wife, David and Melissa Fisher, of the United Church, who took us along home for showers and to do some laundry, treating us like royalty.

Daylight comes early that far north. The sun was already shining in the window when I awoke around 4:30 AM. Of course, the farther north we travel, the longer the daylight hours will be. This may be hard for me, because I tend to wake up with daylight, whereas Glen can sleep right on. I am glad that he can and then feel rested to drive that tractor all day long. A night of only four to five hours of sleep is not enough for this grandma, so I did some serious sleeping while riding on the tractor.

There were days of near tedium on the road. In my journal I wrote, "The miles dragged out past the unending fields of canola, pastures and fields of nothing out to the far horizons. Didn't even see any farm buildings. The weather was sunny."

Then there was also unexpected drama. At Defoe, we pulled into a service station to fill the tractor tank with fuel. After a short distance on the way again, I suddenly began to smell gasoline. At the same time, Glen noticed, to his dismay, that the gas tank cap was missing. Turning around, we retraced our way back to the station, praying that the cap was still there or that someone had found it. Just as we got to the station, Glen saw the bright green object lying on the hard-packed gravel. What a relief! "Thank you, Lord!" we whispered and turned out onto the highway again.

Later in the day, a tour bus caught up with us on Route 17, which is also called the Yellowhead Highway. It swung around us and stopped.

Out jumped the twenty-one passengers with their cameras. Mel and Martha Eby from Waterloo, Ontario were the driver and tour director. Their passengers were Canadians and Americans who were excited about traveling to Alaska. Noticing by our trailer license that we were from Ohio, the Ebys asked if we had ever heard of Dalton. "Yes! That's our address," Glen answered.

"Well, just two weeks ago, we visited our friends, Raymond and Lucile Steiner on Jericho Road near Dalton," remarked Martha. I told them we also live on Jericho Road and know the Steiners. Small world!

In the town of Lanigan we noticed that the slow-moving signal lights were not all flashing, so we checked in with Pat and Elaine Carty, a pastor friend of the church where we had stayed the previous weekend. He called a friend who found the problem. Since it was "Canada Day" (July 1) and no stores were open, he took the flasher unit out of his own vehicle and put it on the tractor, making the repairs. That certainly was "second mile" Christianity!

After a pleasant overnight with the Cartys, Glen turned the tractor out onto the highway again toward Saskatoon. Heavy rains began to fall, obstructing our view of the road signs. Because of this and a construction area, we missed the Route 17 West Circle Road around the large city. Since we had to keep to the center of the highway, traffic slowed down behind us. Finally, we came to an exit where we were able to turn in at a service station and get directions for getting out of the city and back on 17 West again. What a relief it was to get out of the traffic and continue on a secondary road.

At the town of Langham we tried a telephone call to a pastor recommended to us by friends as someone who might be able to find us a place to stay overnight. Since we could not get through to him by phone, we decided to stop at a nearby restaurant to eat a bite and then try again. Glen was getting a little apprehensive since dusk was fast approaching.

While waiting to be served, we noticed a lady seated at the next table enjoying her meal and reading a book. I asked her politely if she was from town and if she knew of a place where we could park for the night.

"Yes, I'm from this place," she said. After talking a bit with us, Gayle Robinson offered, with a friendly smile, "My teacher husband and daughters are on a vacation fishing trip. Our sons are counselors at a Bible camp and I'm all alone. Why don't you come over to my home and park your trailer and tractor there? I have been wondering what I was going to do with myself to pass the time," she laughed.

To add to that provision of kindness, since Gayle is a beautician, she said, "Glen, you need a haircut." She motioned for him to sit down on a kitchen chair and gave him a haircut that evening. Gayle had to leave for her workplace the next morning at 8:45, leaving us to lock up the house when we were ready to leave a bit later. We felt overwhelmed to think that she met us only 15 hours earlier and now trusted us in their beautiful home.

Again I must say, every day we are amazed and grateful for the way the Lord cares for us, our precious families, our church body, and all the wonderful people who are interested in our endeavor. It is so wonderful when Christians can feel the bond of friendship and can trust one another like that.

We traveled through rain most of that day and were happy that the tractor did not seem to mind. Coming to the area of North Battleford, we decided to stop at a Wal-Mart store for a change of pace and to do a little shopping. Also, it was time to begin looking for a place to tie up for the night.

We had been given the name of a couple here who were potential hosts, but we found out that their telephone number was no longer in service. The manager of the Wal-Mart then suggested the David Laird campground nearby as a nice and quiet place for us to spend the night. It turned out to be just as he described it.

As we were returning to the tractor, we were met by a man who just got out of his pickup truck from the John Deere dealership. His smile seemed to display that he was victorious. He said he had heard that we were in the area, so he drove up and down the highway to find us. He happened to glance toward the Wal-Mart parking lot and his search was over. Pat Smith acted as though he was rewarded by taking pictures. The next morning he came to the campground to wish us well.

Leaving North Battleford the next morning, we passed along lush and beautiful rolling hill country. The skies had cleared, and out of a heart filled with joy and praise I sang, "For the beauty of the earth . . ." but only the Lord and I heard it. Wearing earplugs to protect us from the noise of the tractor, Glen was unable to hear it to smile and agree.

Previous to that day, we had heard of a man traveling through Canada on a two-horse hitch pulling a covered wagon. He was raising funds for diabetes research. That day we came upon evidence that he was nearby. We noticed horse "do-do" on the road, sometimes on the right side of the driving lane and next on the left. We spied the wagon parked off the highway. Cecil Philips from Amaranth, Manitoba had unhitched the horses and was grazing them in the grassy area beside the road. After visiting with him briefly, we resumed our journey. Our hearts went out to him. He had lost two wives to cancer and he himself was a diabetic.

With Glen concentrating on the driving, I had a lot of time on my

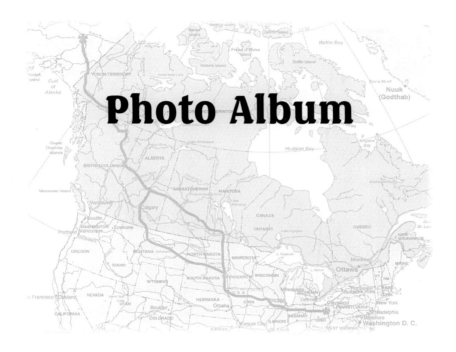

Photo Album

The John Deere tractor before the cab was put on.

The silk rose even became a popular item for photographers.

The tractor team—Glen & Betty Martin.

A spare tire and generator were mounted on the back of the camper "just in case." Note the banner.

A vanload of Amish stopped us near Shepherd's Inn, Fort St. John, British Columbia. They were returning to the States.

Mel and Martha Eby host the group headed for Alaska. The travelers came from Canada and the U.S.

An Alaska farmer gave a tomato and cucumber. We covered the front windows on the camper so they wouldn't be damaged by gravel.

Pausing to view the beautiful Kulane Lake in the Yukon.

Just went through Canadian customs. The tourists we met were Elon Baker and Don Ware from Michigan.

Proof of being in Alaska. It seemed everyone who traveled here stopped to take a picture.

Yukon! Here we come through your wilderness.

Some of the KJNP staff in North Pole. These are dedicated people serving the Lord and getting the Good News out over the airwaves.

Tim Bartholomew, Betty Martin, and Edgar Raber visit under the wide open Montana sky.

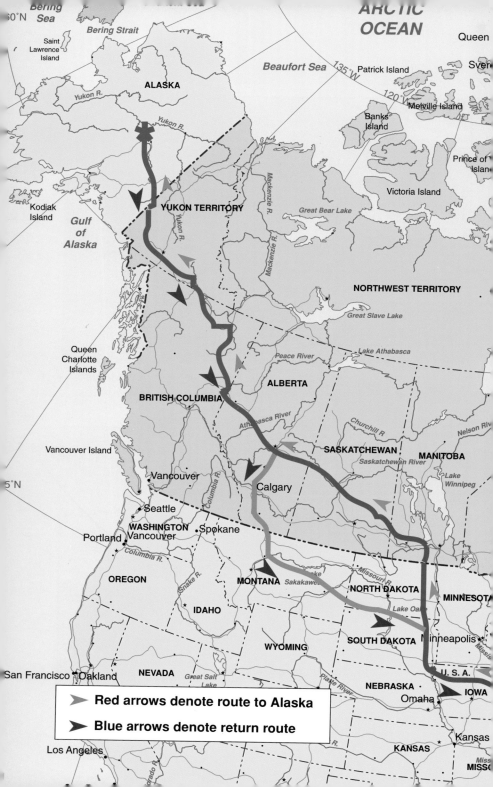

Red arrows denote route to Alaska

Blue arrows denote return route

Syd and Nettie Spiker, Morinville, Alberta, were gracious hosts when we parked by their home in July and September.

The Martins with Muriel and Paul Lang from near Columbus, OH. It was special to meet folks from OH, who became good friends.

Camping friends washed the tractor with water from a nearby lake.

Every now and then Glen had to adjust the clutch, especially after long, hard pulls in the mountains.

The Corn Palace is in Mitchell, SD. Glen thought a photo of the tractor next to the palace would be an agricultural picture.

Just posing for another photographer.

The breakfast at Prophet River was extra good.

Dale and Norma Mollenbeck, Hampton, Iowa, were just two of the many people who invited us to park on their property.

Pictures from second trip - Tetlin Reservation

Roy and Cora David with John Strasser.

Home of the Davids.

Chief Danny,
son of Roy
and Cora.

View of
some
houses
in Tetlin.

Schoolhouse
in Tetlin.

The Story of Jesus

"For God so loved the world that he gave his one and only Son, that whoever believes in him shall not perish but have eternal life."
John 3:16(NIV)

God sent his son, Jesus, into the world as a little baby. His mother was Mary, a virgin. She married Joseph, a carpenter, after she was pregnant with Jesus by the Holy Spirit. It was God, not Joseph, who was the father of Jesus. Jesus was born in Bethlehem, where Mary and Joseph had to go because of a national census in Israel.

Jesus grew up in Nazareth, working in Joseph's carpenter shop. At the age of thirty, after a forty day fast and baptism by John in the Jordan River, Jesus went out at God's direction and began to tell the people about the kingdom of God. He chose twelve close followers whom he taught, and he did many miracles, showing how very much God loved people.

Eventually, out of jealousy over Jesus' popularity with the people, the religious leaders of the day arrested him. They took him to Pontius Pilate. He had Jesus whipped and crucified to satisfy the Jewish officials who had stirred up some of the people against Jesus.

Jesus willingly laid down his life to cover our sins. On the third day, he rose from the dead and is now on the heavenly throne, with God the Father.

At God's appointed time, Jesus will return, raise the dead, judge everyone, and rule forever.

All of us are sinners, according to the Bible, and are headed for eternal separation from God. When we ask Jesus to forgive our sins and to come into our lives as Savior and Lord, he hears us. He removes our sin from us and gives life to our spirit immediately, making us a part of God's family. That life lasts forever. Even though we die, when Jesus comes back to earth from heaven, he will raise up our dead body and make it new, putting our eternal spirit into this new body. And we will live with him forever.

If you want to accept Jesus as your Savior, tell God: "I, (your name), am a sinner. I'm sorry for my disobedience to you, God, and I want to turn away from my sins. I receive Jesus' sacrifice of his life so my sin will be taken away. I receive the eternal life you give in exchange for the death that I deserve. Thank you for making me a part of your family, God."

If you prayed the prayer to receive Jesus Christ as your savior, please let us know.

Write to us at:

Miles for Missions
c/o Lighthouse Christian Fellowship
164 North Washington Street
Millersburg, Ohio 44654

WORLD OUTREACH

"It has always been my ambition to preach the gospel where Christ was not known, so that I would not be building on some else's foundation. Rather, it is written: 'Those who were not told about him will see, and those who have not heard will understand.'"
Romans 15:20,21 (NIV)

PURPOSE

Glen Martin prayed for 18 months for money to help get the gospel to unreached people groups. Then he felt God's guidance to undertake this estimated 15,000 mile tractor trip from Dalton, Ohio, to Alaska and back, to help raise awareness of this need and funds for it. His scriptural basis is:
Romans 15:20,21.

BACKGROUND

Since an encounter with God at age six, Glen has known the call to reach those who have not heard the gospel. In his teens and as a young married man, he traveled to nearby cities to tell the good news to those who had not heard it. Then he began to pray for God's burden for lost souls.

Shortly after, he was in Kidron, Ohio, on business. When the business was completed, an oriental lady who was visiting there stepped forward. She said, "Young man, I have a word for you. There will be a day when you will go all over the world taking God's message."

That began to be fulfilled. While Betty kept things in order at home, Glen made 25 short term mission trips to spread the gospel to those who had never heard it in Haiti and in Asia.

Glen and Betty have been married 45 years. They have four children and fifteen grandchildren.

Travel expenses for the Martins are being funded by their home church, Lighthouse Christian Fellowship, Millersburg, Ohio.

Donated funds will be used for foreign and domestic missions through:

Miles for Missions World Outreach
c/o Lighthouse Christian Fellowship
164 North Washington Street
Millersburg, Ohio 44654

Phone contributions: Toll free **1-888-278-0865**

WORLD OUTREACH

Lighthouse Statement of Faith

We believe:
God is triune. God the Father, God the Son and God the Holy Spirit are one God. Jesus Christ is the only begotten Son of God born of a virgin. He died as payment for sins. He was resurrected from the dead, ascended to heaven, and will come again. The Bible is the infallible Word of God, inspired by the Holy Spirit. The local church is a part of the universal body of Christ.

Follow the Martins on the World Wide Web:

www.milesformissions.org

Yes, I/We would like to take part by pledging the following amount:

Name_____

Address_____

City _____ Zip_____

Estimated 15,000 mile round trip.

- ☐ 1¢/mile ($150)   ☐ 2¢/mile ($300)
- ☐ 3¢/mile ($450)   ☐ 4¢/mile ($600)
- ☐ 5¢/mile ($750)   ☐ 6¢/mile ($900)
- ☐ 7¢/mile ($1,050) ☐ 8¢/mile ($1,200)
- ☐ 9¢/mile ($1,350) ☐ 10¢/mile ($1,500)

Other _____ /Mile

Non-mileage donation $_____

Charge Card Donation Amount $_____

Master ☐   Visa ☐   Discover ☐

Card No. _____

Exp. Date: _____

Authorized Signature:_____

Please make checks payable to:

Miles for Missions
c/o Lighthouse Christian Fellowship
164 North Washington Street
Millersburg, OH 44654

Phone contributions:
Toll free 1-888-278-0865

hands, so I decided to try reading and was pleasantly surprised that I could, in spite of the noise and vibration of the machine as we rolled along. Again nightfall came and we had to look for a parking space. Friends had given us the name of Kevin Olive, pastor of the Lloydminster Gospel Fellowship. His reaction on the telephone was like most others —a hearty laugh when he heard that we were driving a John Deere tractor all the way to Alaska.

This pastor and his wife Lisa welcomed us and arranged for us to park by the church. In the morning, Pastor Olive helped Glen replace the rubber gas line on the tractor and we were off again, headed for Alaska. The city of Lloydminster was built on the Saskatchewan—Alberta line. We slept on the Saskatchewan side of the city.

As we approached a small town, we saw a sign along the way that read: "Folks with a lot of brass are seldom polished." Another read: "The wheel was man's greatest invention until he got behind it."

Alberta ∿ ─────────────────────────
July 4th

Once in Alberta province, we found the towns scattered and farther apart. Rolling along until we came to the village of Vegreville, we found a Ukrainian festival in full swing, with many people in town. Stopping to make a phone call to Pastor Kevin Jamieson, a name given to us by friends on a previous day, we could get no answer, so we pulled in to a Kentucky Fried Chicken restaurant to eat.

We were the only ones in the place when a distinguished-looking gentleman came walking in, gave his order, and sat down. He began talking with us about our mission. When we were ready to leave, he gave us his card that read: "The Honorable Dr. Stephen West, Alberta Minister of Energy." He told us to be sure to call him if we ran into any kind of trouble while traveling through Alberta. We were delighted to have met this friendly provincial official. We pray that God will help us to relate to people in such a way that when they talk to us they too may feel honored—for we are children of the King and represent Him.

After supper we finally made contact with Pastor Jamieson's wife. She told us to meet him at their church at 9:00 PM, which we did. We ended up getting a good night's sleep, grateful for the generous hospitality of so many of the Lord's people along the way. That Sunday morning we worshipped with Pastor Jamieson's congregation. After lunch at a subway shop as guests of Robin and Carol Cruickshank and daughter Christan, we were ready to get on the road again. Then we noticed that one of the trailer tires had a slow leak. Fortunately we were able to find a service station to add air to the tire.

The afternoon was very hot as we continued along, with a lot of traffic on the highway. Many of the vehicles were RV's (recreational vehicles). Syd and Nettie Spiker of Morinville had stopped along the way to rest when they heard the putt-putt of the tractor and saw it go by. Noticing the banner on the trailer and the words across the cab of the tractor, they wondered what this meant.

Catching up with us later on, we developed an immediate bond of friendship because they too are believers. Syd has an equipment business in their town and invited Glen to bring the tractor over to his shop the next day and work on oil seals that were leaking. What a gracious provision this was from the Lord. We parked in their driveway. How great it was to "sleep in" and awaken to a new day, a new place, and a new opportunity. Glen took the tractor to Syd's shop for the repairs needed, while I did some laundry and cleaning in the trailer. That evening we had a tasty meal featuring bison which they raise.

On Tuesday evening, Syd and Nettie invited some friends over for a wiener roast. The July evening was perfect as we shared the purpose of our venture and highlights from the trip thus far with the group gathered around the fire. When I mentioned that we could not talk to each other because the tractor gears were so noisy, one man sighed a bit and said, "I wouldn't mind trying that for a day." That brought out laughter from everyone.

That evening I wrote in my journal, "The Spikers are like angels of mercy to us. We recognize that the Lord has sent many people to us just at the right time. He is faithful!"

I went on to write that I was reminded of the scripture verse in Psalm 133:1 where it says, "How good and pleasant it is for the brethren to dwell together in unity." This was true of our families, in the church body of believers, and in the people we were meeting along the way. "We are so blessed as our circle of friends grows," I wrote. It was the end of a beautiful, inspiring day.

The next day the men at the shop replaced the oil seal on the flywheel and a grease seal on the rear axle, and installed insulation and pieces of carpet in the cab to help deaden the noise. That evening Syd, Nettie, and we were invited to the home of Jon and Esther Bucher for a delightful dinner. They have a beautiful home near Morinville and are U.S. citizens by birth, transplanted from West Virginia and Virginia.

We had been with the Spikers three days and four nights, which made for many fond memories. As we were driving along on Route 37, a TV cameraman flagged us down as we rounded a bend in the road. Glen stopped the tractor for an interview. The man told us that the program would be aired that evening on station CFRN on the 6:00 news hour,

which we did not get to see. The day before we had also been interviewed over the telephone by a radio station reporter on FM 101.9.

Calling ahead early in the morning, we asked permission from the
pastor of the Whitecourt Pentecostal Church to park by his church for
the night. Although they were to be gone overnight, he did give that
permission to us. Setting up our lawn chairs under wide, spreading trees,
we spent a pleasant evening resting and relaxing in the cool shade.

On July tenth, as we were driving along Route 43, a man in a pickup
truck stopped us and handed Glen a baseball cap with the lettering
"Paddy's Oil Service," which was a kind gesture of welcome into Alberta
country. On that day, we saw our first moose along the way—one carved
out of wood, that is! We had not yet seen a live one, but we did see
one deer along the road.

The scenery in northern Alberta was now changing. Instead of acres
and acres of flat, open lands, we were now seeing thousands of pine
trees covering a more rolling landscape. Many of the trees had been
harvested, probably to be turned into newsprint and other paper. One
large area of trees was designated as being owned by a newsprint
company. Along that stretch of road, in the afternoon, a couple from Iowa
stopped us to talk because they farm with John Deere tractors. That
evening we arrived in the village of Valleyview and parked overnight at
Sherk's RV Park. We would give Sherk's an "A" for cleanliness. That
day we had driven 107 miles, with 2,800 the total mileage so far on our
journey from Dalton, Ohio.

In the morning we decided not to push for an early start since the
weather the day before had been very hot and the day was long. After a hearty breakfast at Travelers Restaurant in Valleyview, we got
back on the road and followed it as it turned westward toward Grande
Prairie. In the Crooked Creek area, we noticed several people waving

to us, beckoning us to stop. Neil Holmes had seen us in Valleyview and knew we were heading out past their home. So he, his wife, and grandson were waiting. Neil took Polaroid pictures of us and asked us to autograph them.

Mr. Holmes told us Crooked Creek consisted of a gas station, grocery store, and post office. Sure enough, six miles up the road, we found the building that housed all three facilities. We stopped to contribute to their economy just a little. The women workers were so easy to chat with. One of them quickly made a fresh pot of coffee when she saw that Glen was carrying an empty coffee mug.

Farther along, at another driveway, a man was waiting to get information from Glen for a newspaper article. In all such instances, we handed out our "Miles for Missions" brochures.

While continuing to ride along Route 43 on that Saturday, we passed an intersection where Bob and Ruth Balisky were waiting to pull out on the highway on their way to join their family at a lake for the weekend. Seeing the words on the tractor, they pulled in front of us and stopped to talk. When Bob learned that the one oil seal had begun leaking again, despite the good work done by the Spikers, he invited Glen to take the tractor to the John Deere dealership in Grande Prairie on Monday morning. Glen commented, "Won't that be difficult without an appointment?" Bob kindly informed us that he and his three brothers own the business called Peace Farm Power.

Plans for the weekend developed quickly from there on. Bob called John and Annie Warkentine to make plans for us to park our rig at their home. The Warkentines were very gracious hosts and made us feel right at home. They have 20 grandchildren. Anyone who knows us realizes that "grandchildren" is a very important subject of conversation. In a short time, Annie prepared a delicious meal. One could tell that she had made many meals for their six children and extended family throughout their 50 years of marriage. She was a shining example of a Christian woman.

"This is our sixth Sunday away from home," I wrote in my journal. "We left the Warkentine residence and drove our rig to their church, and they asked Glen to share our vision with the church. There are many farmers in this Bezanson Community Church whose favorite tractor color is green!"

Bright and early on Monday morning, Glen drove the tractor to the Peace Farm Power shop where the men were intrigued by the antique tractor. As he drove Dandelion into the shop, he deliberately made it pop like only the two-popper can do. One of the workers grinned as he shouted, "I love it, I love it, I love it!" They had a machine shop make a custom-made oil retainer that fit perfectly and appeared to finally solve that problem for the tractor. By 5:00 that evening, the repairs were made and Dandelion was ready for the road again. At that time a photographer from a local TV station came along to take photos and for an interview for the satellite channel. A newspaper reporter for a local farm paper also stopped to talk with us, so we were getting good media coverage on this leg of the trip.

After a good night's rest, we faced a cold day on the road. For some unknown reason, the weather had suddenly turned cold and windy, so we had to dress warmly as we rode along Route 43 and then on the Emerson Trail to the home of Terry and Marcy Balisky in the Sexsmith area. They had invited us into their home for supper. After an hour of great fellowship and a delicious meal, we bade farewell to our newfound friends and headed ten miles down the road to the home of David and Ella Loberg, where we were to spend the night.

During the night it began raining, for which the farmers were very grateful. The Loberg's daughter Sonia, and Allen and Louise Heidel-brecht were invited to breakfast at the Loberg's. Allen and Louise had just returned from a trip to Kansas and told how the people who had seen an article in the "Mennonite Weekly Review" there were talking about the couple going from Ohio to Alaska on a tractor. Now they were going to phone their relatives and tell them that they had actually eaten breakfast with the couple on the tractor trip!

British Columbia

July 14th

As we began the day's journey, the rains continued all day, plus the weather also continued to be cold. At 1:30 in the afternoon, a sign wel-comed us into the province of British Columbia. The next sign along the road instructed us to turn back our clock an hour, putting us three hours behind Ohio time.

As we rumbled along, Glen noticed that the muffler on the exhaust stack was wobbling. The vibrations of the many miles had broken the weld. What to do? We kept on traveling until we came to the town of Dawson Creek. Finding a muffler shop, a worker repaired it in a few minutes. Nearly two weeks earlier, a reporter from Dawson Creek had called us and did a write-up about us and our venture in a local paper. The man who repaired the muffler knew that we were coming through his town because he had read about us in that paper.

"We are spending a quiet evening at the Alshart campsite. The woman in charge gave us a less expensive rate because she is so pleased that we stopped here. We are using the turbo heater in the trailer tonight and praying that tomorrow will be warmer. Plans are to get onto the Alaska Highway tomorrow," I wrote in my journal that evening.

In the morning we woke up to the sound of rain. The previous evening TV news carried a spot about us; so people along the way waved at us as we putt-putted by. One couple, Ray and Betty Wickham from Dumont, Iowa just missed us when we had passed through their town in June. Ray and Betty were on their way to Alaska, too, and now were so pleased to meet us in Dawson Creek. However, since Mrs. Wickham was not feeling well, they decided to turn back to Iowa rather than making the trip to Alaska.

The Alaska Highway ～
July 15th

At Dawson Creek, we got on the famous Alaska Highway, or Highway 97. North of Fort St. John the rains stopped, leaving the sky overcast and making the traveling conditions ideal. Many travelers to Alaska stop at the Shepherd's Inn, so we made a stop, too. We had only a cup of coffee then we were back on the road again. Suddenly a gray van coming toward us flashed its lights, so Glen stopped the rig. Out jumped three Amishmen, with their wives following them. To our surprise, one of the couples, the Paul Swartzentrubers, live within a mile of our home in Ohio! Ivan Millers from Sugarcreek and Junior Millers from Wilmot were the other two couples. Jacob Miller, also of Sugarcreek, was the driver of the van. Their visit along the highway provided a very enjoyable interlude for us.

We were coming into different country now as we proceeded on north toward Yukon. The small towns were farther apart along the route, with fewer accommodations available, so we had to keep a careful eye on our fuel supply. This was not the kind of area where one wanted to run out of gasoline for the sturdy little John Deere as it continued faithfully to climb the hills and slopes in sixth gear.

We spent our first night on the Alaska Highway at a camp called "Wonowon" (at mile marker 101). We met many loggers who also spent the night in that camp, and Glen heard one of the men refer to "a bear having been in the camp last night." But it did not bother us. We were probably too weary and in need of a good night's rest to let it trouble us. The lady in charge of the camp refused to take payment for use of the camp from us because "You are on a mission," which was a nice surprise for us.

The following morning we came to a road construction area which slowed us down. After we had driven for awhile, we had to stop in a construction zone and wait for the pilot vehicle. At one point, we were the only vehicle waiting. It seemed the flagger woman hardly knew what to do with us. Finally, a pickup truck with two road workers came and motioned us to go ahead. We imagined the men told the flagger, "Let 'em go—a tractor can easily make it!" We drove alone for a long stretch and when we reached the end of construction, a long line of vehicles was waiting for their turn. There were many smiles and waving hands.

Later in the day we stopped at a restaurant called "Mae's Kitchen". As we were eating bowls of chili and garlic toast, we began discussing where to spend the night. Feelings of frustration began welling up within us. Since getting on the Alaska Highway, there had been few opportunities to talk to people, much less finding parking spaces at churches or homes of Christians. From here on the character of the trip was going to be different. We were heading into wilder, lonelier stretches of country.

Finding a telephone number in a phone book, we called Sikanni River RV Park for an overnight parking place. On the way to that camp we came upon the worst hill of the trip up to that point. The slope over the hill had a nine-percent decline, and I was praying and singing as Glen concentrated on getting the rig to the foot of the hill without mishap. Glen adjusted the clutch on the tractor that evening before turning in. The park had its own generator that made the electricity for the place. Its steady humming lulled us into a well-deserved and restful sleep for the night.

Soon after starting out the next morning, we passed a bicyclist, who then passed us and paused long enough to take a photo of us. At the time Glen thought it would be fun to have a photo of this lonely biker, too. During the day we passed each other several times. Arriving at Prophet River Park, we met the biker, whose name was Rolf and hailed from Germany. He was biking across Canada and did not remember when he last had a shower. He had just been dipping into any river he found along the way, coming back out to soap up, and then back down into the water to rinse off. He fixed his own meals over a campfire, set up a tent to sleep in, and hung up a rope wash line to dry towels, etc. In the morning, after cooking his breakfast and cleaning up, he folded everything up, got on his bike and took off. Two of his friends are flying in from Europe in six weeks to meet him at Anchorage. They will rent a camper there and tour Alaska before returning to Germany again.

While staying at a Provincial Park along the Highway, we met Jim and Judy Lansinger from Kent, Ohio. Their daughter, Laura Murphy, works as a nurse in the eye clinic at Wooster, Ohio, where I had cataract surgery last January. That evening we also met a photographer, David Weaver, from Mansfield, Ohio. These parks have no fees for camping, and have only the bare necessities: one water pump, picnic tables, and two toilets; but no electric hookup.

Waking up to a sunny day was special for us because of all the recent rain. Leaving our bicycle friend, Rolf, and photographer, David Weaver, we drove ten miles to the Prophet River gas station for breakfast and refueling. Then we started out for Fort Nelson. Not long on the road, a van stopped us. The Sam Markels from Ashland, Ohio had read about us seven weeks ago. They assumed that the chances of seeing the tractor people were quite remote, and yet there we were on the highway heading north. The Markels are Christians, and we had a good time visiting and fellowshipping together there along the side of the road.

Word had been getting around through the newspapers, radio, and television about the "Miles for Missions" venture. Another couple from Tulsa, Oklahoma also stopped us. While they had been to Calgary, Alberta at a rodeo they had bought one newspaper and read about this couple from Ohio going to Alaska. They were so excited for the opportunity of seeing us and talking to us about the trip.

Across the many miles on the road, we had been passed by police, sheriffs, and highway patrolmen. They usually waved and went on. But on this particular day we were stopped by a RCMP (Royal Canadian Mounted Police) a few miles south of Fort Nelson. What was his reason for stopping us? We had no license plate on the tractor! What a surprising development that was!

Glen explained that he had inquired of the Highway Patrol in Ohio and they had assured him that a slow-moving vehicle like the John Deere needed no license. But the Mountie explained that without a license, we could have no insurance and that he could fine us up to $1,800 and impound the tractor and trailer unless we could prove to him that we had insurance. The officer said that he would escort us into Fort Nelson where the rig would have to remain until we gave proof of insurance or got a permit from the government to travel onward.

We had made arrangements earlier in the day to spend the night at the Pentecostal HiWay Tabernacle and then worship with them on the morrow. So Glen asked the patrolman if he could escort us to the church and leave the rig there. He agreed, and said he did not want to hinder our mission, but that he had a duty to enforce the law.

Arriving at the church under police escort was a new experience for us, to say the least. We got more attention being escorted by the patrol with flashing lights than if we had entered town on our own! When the pastor came out of the church to meet us, he wondered what on earth had happened. The Mounted Policeman explained the problem. Then he wondered if the pastor and we would say a prayer for his twelve-year-old daughter who was injured and needed corrective surgery. The men promised to pray not only for the daughter, but also for the officer and his wife.

"So here we are at the church," I wrote in my journal. "The pastor gave us the key to the washrooms. It seems evident to us that our being stopped was appointed by God so He could touch the patrolman's entire family!"

Sunday, July 19, we worshiped at the Pentecostal HiWay Church and were thankful to learn that the church office had a fax machine. We called our insurance agent, asking him to fax a proof of insurance certificate to us as soon as possible. Early the next morning I went to the church office and, sure enough, there was a copy of the certificate that we needed to show to the police.

Calvin Shepherd, a local believer and new friend whose workplace was closed for two weeks, had the time to take us around to do some shopping for supplies and then to the police station. At the station an officer made copies of the insurance document, signed the papers, and we were free to go. Was it just a coincidence that the insurance agent was able to fax us the document, that Calvin had free time to help us get around town for our business, and that the police officer was kind and quickly signed the necessary papers? The answer, of course, is a resounding No! Like in so many other incidents, the Lord proved to us that He cared for us and that He was in control!

Facing unpaved, graveled sections of the Alaskan Highway, we had to improvise to protect our trailer windows from rocks and stones that could spin back from our own tractor wheels. Such stones could easily break the windows. So we covered them with cardboard and clear plastic sheets, firmly secured with duct tape. Then, at 2:00 in the afternoon, we headed back out on the highway again.

By this time the "Miles for Missions" venture had gained quite a bit of wide-ranging publicity, which was demonstrated by a couple who flagged us down that afternoon on the road. These people had heard about our trip when we passed through Cherokee, Iowa with the rig on June 15th. Later the couple had flown to Anchorage, Alaska to visit their son and family. While there, they also read about our mission to Alaska in the Anchorage newspapers. Their son was taking them back to Iowa in his RV, and they were so excited to actually meet up with the "Miles for Missions" Martins.

After parking and bedding down at the Tetsa Provincial Park for the night, we left and drove through many miles of forlorn and rather lonely countryside, with a dusty road and mountainous terrain. Over the past few days, we had met Rolf, the German bicyclist. However, three days had passed since we had last seen him. We began wondering if we would ever see him again. Then on this day as we were putt-putting up the mountain Glen saw a familiar looking biker up ahead. It was Rolf! He was having trouble with wheel spokes, but declined the offer for a ride to the next service station. He was determined to solve his problems and ride every inch of the way.

After a hard day of driving, we heard of a camping area owned by Dan and Vicki Clements. There we found pleasant accommodations in their Poplars Campground and Café. Here we met two couples on motorcycles who were members of a Christian biking club from Illinois and Michigan. When we mentioned our dilemma of not knowing the locations of gas stations and campsites, one of the bikers, Russell Lauderback, offered us his copy of the *Milepost*. This is a detailed travel manual for the Alaska Highway that lists every creek, campsite, gas station, eating place, etc. It is an absolute must for overland travelers to Alaska.

Hours later, as we were seated in the Poplars Café, the door opened and in walked Rolf. He had succeeded in making the repairs on his own. That evening we enjoyed visiting with him, as well as with Nancy Larocque and her ten-year-old son Keith from Alberta.

Much to Glen's delight, we finally saw some animals along the way. A variety of different mountain sheep of all sizes, as well as some young elk, were beginning to come into sight. Glen wondered if the tractor noise was keeping the animals from staying along the road. The road was taking us increasingly through mountains and slowing down our progress. On that particular day we covered only 61 miles instead of the 100 miles we had been trying to travel in a day.

The next forenoon, we drove along Muncho Lake. It was truly awesome and beautiful! At the rest area, we met Rolf again. Just before we left, a family came walking toward the tractor. It was a pleasant surprise to see Pastor Peter Stewart, his wife Melody, and their two daughters from the church in Ft. Nelson where we were "impounded."

We could enjoy that beauty for miles, but then we had to climb mountains again. We crossed the Lower Laird River Bridge, the only suspension bridge on the Alaska Highway. Just fifty feet from where we were preparing to turn into the Laird River Lodge for the night, a driver from a camper coming in the opposite direction flagged us down. "I have a message from Tim Beck at the town of North Pole in Alaska. They want you to park the rig at their home when you arrive," he said. He gave Glen their address and phone number. Then he was on his way again. The Becks, who were formerly from Ohio, had heard of the "Miles for Missions" venture and were eager to meet us.

At this Laird River Provincial Park no electric was available, but we spent the night sleeping in our little Argosy trailer. It was a bit hard to think we had to pay to park in an open field with no accommodations. We had a better day in that we drove 72 miles, giving us a total of 3,456 miles so far on the trip.

We headed back out on the road again at 9:30, which was later than usual for us. We steered the tractor toward Coal River and Fireside, which was only 37 miles along the way, but we discovered both places had only gasoline pumping services, no café or camping facilities. The same was true when we arrived at Contact Creek along the Highway, so we had no choice but to keep on putt-putting along. Circumstances change in these places, so the *Milepost* can hardly keep up from year to year.

Yukon Territory ~

July 23rd

At 6:15 that evening, we entered into the Yukon Territory and, a little later, arrived at the Iron Creek Lodge, which had all of the needed facilities available. We felt rewarded to find such a place after having traveled 97 hard miles that day. Before leaving the next morning, we had an interesting conversation with the owner, Vern Hinson, who moved his family there four years ago from Newfoundland and now operates the camp.

In Watson Lake we tried to call a pastor to see if we could park by his church, but there was no response to our call. In checking the *Milepost* we found Green Valley Park only seven miles out of town. When we arrived, we met Rollin and Sharon Cooper from Van Wert, Ohio, who were returning from Alaska. They had read about our trip in an Alaskan paper and were glad to be able to meet us.

This trip was our first experience in using a travel trailer, and I soon learned not to throw any plastic bags or twisties away. Also, it is important to have plenty of paper towels along. We learned the value of having plastic jugs of good water in the trailer. My electric skillet and a one-burner hotplate would have been handy to have along for preparing meals.

"But we are enjoying the trailer so much. Even having the same bed to sleep in each night is special. Today the weather was nice for traveling. It has cooled down, so we were able to sleep well last night," I wrote in my journal on July 24th. Last month Elaine Carty gave us several copies of the *Christian Reader.* I have read all of them while riding on the tractor. They provide inspirational reading. We have also been enjoying *Is That Really You, God?* by Youth With a Mission founder, Loren Cunningham.

We have met people who ask us to pray for them. What an honor that is! We have a list of prayer requests that we pray over daily as we ride along on the road. There is a great number and variety of prayer needs, and the Lord hears, understands, and answers.

"Glen is reading a *Christian Reader Magazine* this evening, which is unusual for him. Often he is weary from driving the tractor when we stop. I have told him that sometimes he wakes up in the evening just in time to go to bed. Glen has the God-given talent to drive that tractor, whether it is up the hills or down the steep mountain slopes. I am so grateful for the way he can navigate the rig!" (Taken from my journal)

Watson Lake is a fascinating place because of its "Sign Post Forest." More than 37,000 signs of places, people's names, and where they are from decorate an area along the highway. From there on we had excellent driving conditions with the exception of two miles where the road was being repaired. Because of the lack of traffic, the 66 miles we traveled that day were pretty lonely. A couple from Michigan stopped us, though. The man knew what it was like riding a tractor cross-country. In 1979 he had joined a band of disgruntled farmers who rode their tractors to Washington D.C. to get the government's attention.

Another man by the name of Dave Anderson, who was hauling a Massey-Ferguson tractor on a trailer, also stopped. Laughing heartily, he said, "Excuse me for laughing, but this is something I have never seen on this highway!" Before parting, Anderson told us that he gets the *Lehman Hardware Catalogue* from Kidron, Ohio, which is only five miles from our home. That night we slept at Rancheria, a roadside combination of gas station, café, and camping and parking facilities.

The next day was Sunday, July 26th, and the first Sunday on our trip that we were unable to attend a church service. Driving along these lonely stretches of road on the Alaska Highway, we sometimes had to wonder where the people were. The weather was ideal again for traveling that day, and we made the first stop of the day at the Continental Divide Restaurant for breakfast. We enjoyed watching the owners' twin ten-year-old grandchildren, Brittney and Bridgett, from Edmonton, Alberta, who helped in the restaurant and store. They were good, cheerful kids and brightened up the atmosphere of the place. They had seen the rig from their school bus when we traveled through their area almost a month before!

Driving 43 miles farther that day, we came to our destination for the night at Morley River, a camp with no electrical hookup. As we were parking, a fellow by the name of Larry Wynnyk came up to talk with us. A friend back in Morinville had told him that if he ever sees an antique John Deere tractor on the highway, he should be sure to stop and talk with the couple. Larry was a dedicated Christian and a real encouragement to us as he shared with us how God had answered some of his prayers.

The Morley River Lodge advertised in the *Milepost* that they had an artesian water well, so we filled four gallon jugs with fresh water. The next morning, after taking time to adjust the clutch on the tractor, we turned back out onto the highway at 8:45 and continued the journey. Twenty-three miles later we crossed a very long bridge into the town of Teslin, but we kept on traveling until we came to Mukluk Annie's Salmon Bake. A busload of tourists had passed us on the road and was waiting to take photos when we pulled in at Mukluk. We had a delicious meal of salmon and celebrated my 67th birthday there in Yukon Territory on July 27th.

Back on the road again, we reached our goal for the day by arriving at Jake's Corner by 5:30 that evening. The proprietor had all kinds of antiques piled around the place: old tractors, trucks, etc. Dave and Laureen Gilbert manage the gas station and restaurant. The food was extra good, and we decided that their breakfast was the best of any restaurant along the way thus far. The Gilberts' kindness was demonstrated as they refused payment for the meals. We had to stay in one of their motel rooms because they had no camping facilities.

By this time, we were getting far enough north that the daylight hours were beginning to stretch into a longer span. We were getting adjusted to falling asleep while it was still daylight and waking up again in the daylight with only a few hours of darkness between.

One of the marvels of the trip was how God kept bringing the right people along at the right time for special needs. In the morning, before leaving Jake's Corner, Glen took the tractor clutch assembly apart to inspect it. On a long trip of this nature, such maintenance was very necessary. Larry and Jean Soucy from Fort St. John, British Columbia, just "happened" to come along while Glen was working on the tractor. They came over to where Glen was working and introduced themselves. Since Larry is a mechanic, Glen very much appreciated Larry's assuring him that the clutch assembly looked as though the lining parts were all in good condition.

The drive toward Whitehorse was interesting because we saw many side roads winding through the trees, with glimpses of houses and other buildings. We saw more of such during this four-hour stretch of road than we had along all of the Alaska Highway up to that time. However, we did not want to turn and go into Whitehorse proper since we wanted to stay close to the highway.

We had two leads on pastors to call for possible parking for the night. On the first call we learned from a daughter that her parents were not at home. With the second, we had no clue where that church might be, so we stopped at a small convenience store nearby. When Glen asked the cashier if she knew of a church in the area, she said, "Yes, there is one in sight of the store over there called 'The Yukon Bible Fellowship' and the pastor lives right next to the church."

What a wave of relief and joy spread over us as we drove over to the church. We were barely down from the tractor when a pickup truck came wheeling into the parking lot behind us and the driver said, "I have a tractor just like that one in my yard!" The same man came to the meeting at the church later that night.

Once again, God's timing was perfect for us. The next morning, July 29th, Pastor Mark Bernard took Glen to several stores for some supplies. Prices soared there in the Yukon! Glen had purchased a gallon of Aloe Vera juice in Ohio at Wal-Mart for $6.95 and in Saskatchewan for $16.95, but on that afternoon he had to pay $41.80 for a gallon of the juice. Shawna, the pastor's wife, made a nice lunch for us, after which we bade the Bernards good-bye. By 1:25 we were back on the highway toward Alaska again.

Now we were heading into the longest stretch of road without any gas stations—between Whitehorse and Otter Falls, so we were prepared with an extra container of gas. The tractor gas tank did get empty, so we were thankful for the extra can. That was a lonely 78-mile stretch of road.

Stopping at Otter Falls, we were the only campers at this lonely outpost. We had heard that the Yukon news media out of Whitehorse wanted to do an interview, so Glen called them. They arranged for a reporter and photographer to catch up with us along the road. Later, when the news people met us and were talking with us, Art and May Joy Adolphson from Valleyview, Alberta drove up. In addition to being interested in the tractor, they also wanted to know about our mission.

The Adolphsons had a challenging mission. With a love and burden for the people in the far north, they routinely take videos on the life and ministry of Jesus, as well as other Christian literature, with them. Going from door to door in the villages, they give copies of the Jesus video and Gospel tracts by Billy Graham to the people in these isolated places.

When they mention Billy Graham's name, the eyes of the people usually light up and they want the literature. That far north the people do not have television, but they do have video playing equipment. Meeting Art and May Joy with their unique vision and dedication turned into a real inspiration and encouragement to us.

The reporter from the *Yukon News* also seemed captivated by the Adolphsons' testimony and included them in his interview with us. "We trust that he has written the truth so that tomorrow's newspaper will carry at least two positive articles about what God is doing!" (That line was jotted in my journal.)

The following day on the road the weather was getting cloudy and colder. We stopped in Haines Junction at a place called Cozy Corner. The cooks suggested the Snag Junction Campground as a better site.

Driving into that campground, we were met by Armond and Sharon Martineau from Valley Center, California and Bernie and Barbara Jahn from New Brighton, Minnesota. The next morning, to Glen's surprise, Armond and Bernie got busy and cleaned off the rest of the road mud from the rig for us.

Armond was so fascinated with the John Deere. While still in Alaska, he heard on the news that a John Deere tractor was on its way to Fairbanks. As a young boy he had learned to drive a tractor, so he hoped they would meet us somewhere on the highway. Sure enough, at Snag Junction they heard the old familiar sound of the putt-putting of the trusty old John Deere in the distance. He got really excited, hoping it would be us—and it was! We had a grand time with these two couples at that camp. "You not only made my day—you made my trip!" exclaimed Armond as we parted the next day.

Eight

August 1st

*"He told them, the harvest is plentiful,
but the workers are few. Ask the Lord of the harvest,
therefore, to send out workers into His harvest field." Luke 10:2*

AT TWO O'CLOCK WE ROLLED over the Alaska line and then, eighteen miles farther down the highway, we pulled up to the U.S. Customs office referred to in the beginning chapter of this book. The time in Alaska is four hours behind Ohio time, which made it hard to call family and friends at a decent hour, although it stayed daylight most of the time. We called anyway, so the people back home could rejoice with us for the safe journey to our destination.

Hunting up the Lakeview Campground, recommended to us by Armond and Sharon who had slept there two nights before, we parked the rig for our first night in Alaska. This was a beautiful scenic spot along a clear, calm lake. As a bonus for Glen, we saw that first large wild animal—a big bull moose along the highway.

While stopping along the highway that afternoon, we met a young couple from Minnesota and their six-year-old daughter Bailey. The little girl had a quarter that she was saving up to give to some special cause, so she decided to give it to "Miles for Missions" and, as you can imagine, this really touched our hearts. Another Martin couple from Lancaster, Pennsylvania stopped at the same time to talk with us. Every time that it was appropriate to do so, we witnessed to the people about the Lord and our mission, believing that the Lord was going to honor our vision and burden for missions.

As we traveled on the Alaska Highway, we often drove many miles without meeting another vehicle. At times we wondered if we were the only ones headed for Alaska. Then our thoughts were diverted as several campers passed us. We waved to oncoming drivers, thinking they probably passed us a week or two ago, had their Alaskan vacation, and were on the homeward trail. They found us still putt-putting along. Many times I thought, "Oh well, we're going to make it sometime!"

The time came that one of the trailer tires had to be repaired or replaced. According to the *Milepost,* we would find a service station six miles down the road. Yes, we found it, but no repairman was there. The young woman cashier said Glen could use the air hose. She noticed the words on our tractor and wondered what we were all about. I gave her a brochure to read and then we went next door to have breakfast at a restaurant.

We were the only customers at the restaurant. While we were leisurely enjoying the meal, the door opened and a woman's voice said, "There they are!" Merlin and Fay Christianson from Riceville, Iowa had talked with us nineteen days ago, gone to Alaska, and were now heading home. They said they were thinking about us that very morning and then noticed our parked rig. It was an enjoyable time of "catching up."

We needed to return to the gas station to use the telephone. The cashier told us that as a child, she thought she would want to be a missionary. In her teen years she and her mother left Florida and moved to Alaska. She lost her zeal to serve the Lord and now regrets it, stating that she and her husband are not attending church at all. Reading the brochure reminded her of her past desires. Our prayer is that her love for the Lord will be rekindled. It reminded us how easy it is to become distracted and get our priorities mixed up.

That morning before we had started traveling, Glen prayed that the Lord would enable us to have many people contacts. The ministry to that girl was an answer to his prayer.

The first town we came to in Alaska was Tok. As we stopped in the parking lot of Fast Eddy's, a popular restaurant, many people were wandering around and in a moment, they came walking toward us to talk and take pictures. It was hard to believe that so many people could surround us so quickly. Six women from Georgia had passed us a few miles back and now they wanted to see Dandelion and us in "still life." Others looked on and took pictures without getting acquainted.

One of the couples waited around so they could talk with us for sure. Two weeks earlier, Harold and Lois Gingrich from Fredericksburg, Pennsylvania left their country home for Alaska. On the way out the drive, they stopped to get the mail. One of the items was the *Farm and Dairy* with an article entitled *"Ohio to Alaska . . . Nothing Runs like a Deere"* which included a photo of the rig and the Martins.

The Gingriches said, "Wouldn't it be interesting if we'd see them on our trip!" They saved the paper and kept watching for us. They found us in Fast Eddy's parking lot and after getting acquainted, asked if we'd want the article. This was of much interest to us because we had seen very little media coverage of the venture. Harold and Lois invited us to eat with them. What a pleasant experience! All his life, Glen has been familiar with the *Farm and Dairy*. It is published in Salem, close to his childhood home area.

Paul and Muriel Lang, from Pataskala, Ohio had their truck camper on a farm wagon for winter storage. They had plans to go to Alaska. When it was time to get it out of the machinery shed, Paul used one of his John Deere tractors to pull it out. Muriel was watching him and came up with the novel idea of suggesting (just in fun) that they could drive the John Deere to Alaska. Paul looked at his wife in amazement and replied, "Oh my, we couldn't get that accomplished in our lifetime!"

They made it to Tok, Alaska in their truck camper. Paul was waiting in the truck while Muriel was making a reservation for the night at the Bull Shooter RV Park. Paul thought he heard the two-popper sound. Could it possibly be a John Deere? He looked in the direction of the sound and as we came closer, he wished Muriel would hurry so they could follow us down the street. They soon found us at the gas station.

The Langs pulled in behind us and discovered we were from Ohio. At this point in time, the Langs and Martins became acquainted and a lifetime friendship was begun. We also spent the night at the Bull Shooter. As we were visiting, a couple on a motorcycle stopped to check out the tractor people. Robert and Nancy Gasser were fun-loving people from California.

Two other visitors that night were Pastor Terry and Grace Brigner, who came to Tok from Michigan twenty-five years ago. He is pastor of the "Chapel of the North." They kindly offered help for whatever we might need.

Traveling along that day out of the village of Tok, a man stopped us to give us a large tomato and a cucumber. "I want you to enjoy some of our produce," he said with a smile. What a kind gesture. The fresh vegetables were so tasty.

We found only one service station and restaurant on the 82-mile stretch of road. The Langs passed us on their way to Delta Junction and the Gassers, our motorcycle friends, passed us with North Pole as their destination. That night we came to a free campground that friends had recommended. The Grestle Camp was a very quiet place. A biker in a tent, a big camper RV, and we were the only ones taking refuge there for the night.

At one construction area, the flagger told us to follow right behind the pilot car so we would not get so much dust in our cab. We felt that drivers treated us with respect. We had heard that there is always road construction in progress in Alaska because of permafrost conditions. It was good to get to a gas station and walk around. A sign on the door informed customers, "Sorry, no washrooms."

Among the many interesting people we met on the trip was a grand-mother, Brenda Peterson, and her granddaughter who introduced themselves to us when they had stopped at a lodge to make phone calls. The women were excited about their move from Missouri to Delta Junction, Alaska, where the Petersons had purchased 1,200 acres to begin small—grain farming.

Many days ago, someone had told us to be sure to eat at Rika's Road-house in the Big Delta State Park. When we arrived, the first people we saw were Paul and Muriel Lang. By now, we are like family. When we parted, we planned to meet again at North Pole the following day.

From there we had planned to travel on to the next gas station, camp, and then drive on to the town of North Pole the following forenoon. To our dismay, when we arrived at that station, there were no overnight facilities available, leaving us no choice but to continue on. Tim and Debb Beck of North Pole were the ones who had invited us to park at their home. So Glen called to inform them of our plans. This meant 32 miles—two hours—of putt-putting. We arranged to meet them at the North Pole information center.

Around nine o'clock, we made it safely to the center and had to use the telephone at a nearby restaurant-lounge. A number of people who had had plenty of drinks came out to make their remarks about the tractor and the trip. At first they could not believe Glen drove all those miles, but we persuaded them of the truth. Then they shook Glen's hand and congratulated him. We gave a brochure to each person.

The Becks and their daughter Hannah arrived and led us to the Christian radio station where we were able to park and have access to their guesthouse, "the Marriott." Glen drove Dandelion 119 miles that day.

Debb Beck's parents, Jim and Ethel Cotton, are from Creston, Ohio. Ethel had sent the Becks the local newspaper article which accounts for the invitation to their home. The Becks and Cottons are now our friends.

The next morning we met many of the KJNP (King Jesus North Pole) staff, who were very gracious and hospitable. This station has been on the air in Alaska since October 11, 1967 as a 50,000 watt AM station. In 1977, the 25,000-watt FM station was added. Through a series of miracles, they also were able to introduce the TV Channel 4 on December 7, 1980. The history of KJNP is extremely interesting. Don Nelson and his wife Gen were the founders. Since Don's death in 1997, Gen is president and director. She is assisted by Vice President Dick Olson, whose wife Bev is director of programming.

The Becks gave us their pickup truck to use. That was such a blessing! Because of the town name (North Pole), the stores along the strip specialize in Christmas and Santa Claus. Outgoing mail is stamped "North Pole", which, of course, is a novelty and interesting to many people. That noon we ate at Santa's Kitchen. We decided to try Santa's Omelette, which turned out to be a good choice. Since we had been interviewed by a reporter just the day before, we checked the newspaper in the restaurant and found an article and photo of us. Glen told the waitress and she quickly told three couples at a nearby table. They were from Pennsylvania and Delaware. It seemed all of them started talking at once. They went outside, bought three papers, and asked me to autograph them. When we went to pay for our meals, the waitress asked, "Would you please autograph my copy, too?" We certainly did not feel like celebrities.

As planned, we met the Langs at KJNP. I wonder if we'll meet again before all of us return to Ohio.

It was pleasant and unusual not to be traveling the next day and adding to the miles. That evening we drove the rig to the church and worshiped at the North Pole Missionary Chapel nearby. It was a very enjoyable and refreshing time with Pastor Newton and the Lord's people. We spoke in their service to explain the reason for our trip, then gave time for them to ask questions. Many of the people had relatives in Ohio. One fellow had visited his grandmother recently who lives on Jericho Road, not far from our home.

Glen decided the next morning (August 6) to accept Tim Beck's invitation and take the tractor to the Tanana State Fair at nearby Fairbanks to display it for interested people. In the afternoon, we took the tractor to the fairgrounds. A Channel 11 TV reporter came and interviewed us, as well as a reporter from the local Fairbanks newspaper. That evening we were interviewed by Dick Olson on KJNP's TV station where we had the opportunity to talk about "Miles for Missions" for almost thirty minutes of live coverage.

The next days were a whirl of activities for us, with Glen talking to people at the fairgrounds (despite days of steady rain) as well as being entertained by a variety of people and social activities in the Christian community. Local people said it *always* rains during the state fair. While at the fair, a man explained to Glen that he was one of the road construction workers we passed a few days earlier. He said he likes John Deere tractors and when we came along, he shut off his equipment and just listened to the two-popper sounds until we were out of sight. "I loved it!" he commented.

A young boy there at the fair looked at Glen, then asked the question, "Were you ever on TV?"

It took a moment for Glen to recall the recent TV interview, but he answered, "Yes, I was."

"Well, then it *was* you I saw," said the smiling lad.

We went to the post office in North Pole. When we returned to our trailer, I reached into my pocket, but the trailer key was not there. It took only a few minutes to return to the post office. We searched the parking lot and inside the post office without success. I tried hard not to push the panic button as I prayed. A wave of relief swept over me when a postal worker came out to us and asked, "Is this the key you're looking for? A man found it on the lobby floor."

On Saturday night there was a gathering of Native Indians, Eskimos, and anyone who was interested in singing, giving a testimony, or just listening to the exciting experiences of others. This is a weekly meeting that is broadcast live on the radio from their chapel. People came from far and near for this time of inspiration. A young, blind Eskimo man, accomplished vocally and on the guitar, was a special blessing to all of us that night.

We were told that no matter how cold it gets, people continue to come on Saturday nights for "Village Voice." It begins at ten o'clock and ends around midnight. We did not see anyone fall asleep or even yawn. This was a highlight of our time at KJNP.

On Sunday evening, we had an enjoyable visit with Bill and Alma Garner of Glendale, Arizona. They had been in Kidron, Ohio with relatives, Ivan and Joyce Weaver, and kept track of our travels via the Internet. Now the Garners were pleased to meet us, as well as spend time with their daughter and family at Fairbanks (the Mark Carpenter family). Tim, Debb, and Hannah Beck, and Gary and Marissa Jennings also stopped in to bid us farewell.

Nine

August 10th

"But you will receive power when the Holy Spirit comes on you;
and you will be my witnesses in Jerusalem,
and in all Judea and Samaria,
and to the ends of the earth." Acts 1:8

THE MORNING OF AUGUST 10TH ARRIVED calm, clear, and pleasant in Alaska. We were refreshed from a good night's rest. Now it was time for us to say farewell to our friends at KJNP. What a precious gift these and many others along the way had been to us! It was time to turn that faithful antique John Deere around and face the long journey back. After calling each of our children and Dave Christner back in Ohio, who took all of our trip updates, we prayed together with our friends, and drove out onto the Alaska Highway. We left North Pole at nine o'clock that morning for the return to Ohio.

We were not on the road long before a man stopped us to give words of encouragement. This man had left Tallmadge, Ohio in 1970 and came to Alaska to plant a Wesleyan Methodist church in the town of North Pole. Later in the morning, when filling the gas tank at Salche, a couple stopped to tell us that they had just seen us on the Fox TV Channel 7 which informed the viewers that the Martins were starting their journey home. We couldn't imagine how the word had spread so quickly.

To add to the novelty of the day, a bit farther down the road two excited people stopped us, saying that they wanted to give us something. They pulled out a pink salmon fish that they had just caught. They were on a fishing trip and wanted us to have it. I thanked them heartily for their kindness, but never having prepared fresh fish before, I did not quite know what to do with it. Later on in the evening, we asked the owner of the Green Acres Campground where we were staying if she would prepare the fish and share it with us. She declined because of lack of time, but she loaned her electric skillet and lemon pepper. I had cooking oil along. Glen cut it up and I fried it. The result was a delicious supper. We are never too old to learn, eh?

The news coverage was certainly paying off with all of the attention we were getting and opportunities of making new friends. The tractor was performing well, as usual. We put eighty-six miles behind us that first day. We began the return trip with our hearts filled with praise for the many good experiences thus far.

All day it seemed unusual to be driving south instead of north. We were turning the pages of the *Milepost* manual backwards as we were planning each day's trip. This meant that we were finally heading home.

One day we heard about two girls who were traveling in a truck. While listening to Paul Harvey on the radio, they heard with amused interest his telling about a couple from Ohio driving an old John Deere tractor all the way to Alaska and back. A short time later, these girls were surprised and delighted to see us putt-putting along.

The Holy Scriptures speak of the depths of the human heart, a depth that cannot be measured. That depth is rooted in the awesome immensity of God Himself, our Creator. Out of these depths come the capacities and the needs for friendship and fellowship. One of the benefits of this trip for us was the meeting and making of new friends along the way. Again and again both of us noticed how the Lord brought not just curious, but friendly people across our paths. People were truly interested in our "Miles for Missions" venture. People encouraged us in our desire to raise missions awareness and funding. This served as continuing inspiration for our many, many miles of travel.

"There is only one gas station between Delta and Tok," I wrote in my journal. "The day of driving seemed very long, and when I checked the mileage at the end of the day, I realized why. We had gone 94 miles. The tractor performed great today as it climbed the many hills. Each day we are thankful for Dandelion, the powerful old John Deere!"

The following evening as we pulled into a camp along Moon Lake, we noticed several young fellows with cameras. They were in their early twenties. After introductions, we learned that those four young men were from Switzerland. Handing them brochures about our mission, I explained why we were driving that rig all the way to Alaska and back. A short time later the boys returned and gave a generous amount of money as a gift for the mission project. The boys said that they were Christians and were interested in missions and missionaries. It was so interesting to converse with them about their country, jobs, the high cost of living, college, etc. All had the last name of Wieland. Meeting them was the highlight of the day.

Moon Lake was so beautiful with reflections of the trees. The clouds were a perfect reminder of God's creation. It is hard to find words to describe the beauty as the moon shone on the lake.

On August 12th, we began looking for someone along the way who could repair an electrical problem in our trailer. After stopping at one place in Tok, a man in a pickup truck came up to us. He introduced himself as Roy David, a Native from the Tetlin Reservation, who said he liked our missions emphasis. Roy asked us to come to his village "now". Glen said it would not be possible now because the weather was getting colder earlier than usual. We needed to keep moving south and east. But his sincerity worked on our hearts and a divine appointment was made that day for Glen and a team from our church to return to his village for a visit no one would ever forget.

It was evident that the mechanics at the auto repair where we stopped were too busy to help us, but we got acquainted with two couples from Hot Springs, Arkansas—Ray and Annette Stanage and Don and Belva Burroughs—who had encountered radiator trouble five days earlier on their RV. They were still waiting for parts to arrive, which would take several more days. So Ray and Don started checking the trailer's electrical system and were able to repair the problem. We three couples by this time had developed a good friendship and enjoyed lunch together at the Loose Moose Restaurant. There was lots of hearty laughter as the hot peppers turned out to be extra hot!

We pulled in at the Bull Shooter to camp for the night, while the Stanages and Burroughs slept in their RV. Later in the evening Ray came to the trailer to make sure that the electricity was working properly. That was surely going the second mile.

On August 13th we traveled the last 86 miles from Alaska to the Yukon border. When we got to the Border City we filled the tractor tank with gasoline and camped there for the night. The next morning the owner said, "The gas and overnight expenses are on the house." Again we could say, "Thank you, Jesus."

People were always taking pictures of us and our unusual way of travel. Some stopped way ahead of us and then took snapshots of us as we passed by. Others just took pictures as they passed us on the road. But the real enthusiasts, especially ones from Ohio, even flagged us down to stop and talk. One day there were a number of campers that had pulled into a rest area and we saw seven people lined up with cameras as we putted along. One tourist bus drove beside us very slowly so the riders could take photos of us.

Ten

August 14th

*"Unlike so many, we do not peddle the Word of God for profit.
On the contrary, in Christ we speak . . . with sincerity,
as men sent from God." II Corinthians 2:17*

Canada ～

TWENTY MILES DOWN THE ROAD from the Alaskan border
we stopped at the Canadian customs office. The officer in
charge said, "Yes, we heard you were coming. I had read about
it in the *Yukon News.*" With little delay, he waved us through
the station and we were on our way again.

We were back in the Yukon Territory and in the Yukon time zone,
a three-hour difference from Ohio time. Yukon is a rather wild area of
some 207,076 square miles with a population of only 27,979 people.
It is mountain country, with a broad central plateau and has miles of
unexploited forests, wide, sweeping grasslands, and tundra in the north-

ern part of the Territory. The Alaska Highway crosses the southwestern part of the Territory. Most people know a little about the Yukon from the history books because of the gold that was discovered in the Klondike River region in 1896, which triggered a mad gold rush.

We enjoyed stopping in at the Cooks' Koidern River Lodge where Jim and Dorothy have been serving the tourist trade for 30 years. They get their mail only on Mondays, Wednesdays, and Fridays. Dorothy is an excellent cook, but said, "We are just plain tired!" They had saved the *Yukon News* for us, which had a front-page picture of us and a long article. Oh, my!

The Alaska Highway was in much better condition than it had been two weeks earlier, when it was so rough and muddy. Dust had replaced the mud, but we much preferred the drier surface. The weather continued to be pleasant and some of the scenery breathtaking. We stopped to take photos of the majestic mountain range with its cover of snow, a truly magnificent background scene for us as we drove along.

We stopped that night at Cottonwood RV Park along beautiful Lake Kluane. As we walked into the office to register, the girl at the desk said, "When we heard that you were coming, we decided to let you stay for free. We read about you in the *Yukon News* and were hoping you would stop here." They didn't ask us to advertise for them, but we can highly recommend it.

That evening Glen adjusted the clutch and put new pads on the plate to prepare it for the climbing we faced the next day on the road. A tourist from Michigan, who owns fifteen John Deere tractors and was staying at the camp, came and helped Glen.

Since there were no churches in sight, we spent Sunday driving. We stopped in at the Bay Shore Inn again as we had on the way north. The woman was all smiles and wanted to know all about the trip. She had a white ferret on a leash and explained what nice pets ferrets make. She fed it cat food. Domesticated ferrets are an albino variety of the European polecat and hunters used to like them for hunting because they are very adept at sneaking through underground burrows to chase out rabbits and other game.

It was lunchtime so we stopped at the Mackintosh Lodge. One of the customers came to us and said he was the reporter who wrote up our story in the *Yukon News* on July 31st. Yes, we remembered him and could tell him the article was well written.

We stopped for a few minutes at a rest area and were followed by a camper vehicle. The couple, who wanted to meet us, were Lloyd and Norma Weaver of Rochester, Indiana. It was a blessed time of visiting. Soon another RV stopped. This one was a very long bus with "land yacht" printed on it. The couple was from England and had their RV shipped over so they could travel in Canada and America. We saw a real variety of campers.

We arrived in Otter Falls at 5:30. I wrote in my journal: "I must admit thinking that this was going to be a long, quiet evening. I kind of mumbled to the Lord and asked Him to send some people along for the evening so that we can visit. Later, a camper did pull in. What a pleasure to meet Carlton and Nancy Baker from Asheville, North Carolina. Carlton, a retired minister, helps in the seminar ministry at the Billy Graham Center east of Asheville known as "The Cove."

This area through which we were traveling at that time was bear country. Someone told us that there were at least six bears to every Yukon resident, but we had not seen one bear along the road, which was a keen disappointment to Glen. He was determined to see at least one bear on the trip.

Just before we left the camp the next morning, Carlton Baker came up to us with two Bible verses to take along on the road: *"May the God of hope fill you with all joy and peace as you trust Him, so that you may overflow with hope by the power of the Holy Spirit." (Romans 15:13)* and *"Let us not become weary in doing good, for at the proper time we will reap a harvest if we do not give up." (Galatians 6:9).* These two verses were very meaningful as we pondered them on the road that day, for we had to travel a stretch of 78 miles with no gas stations or restaurants to break the monotony. Carlton's parting words to us were, "May you have joy for the journey."

As we approached Whitehorse, the capital of Yukon, a man stopped us on the road, shook Glen's hand and, to his surprise, gave him a five-dollar bill. He was not wearing a shirt and said energetically, as if to defend himself, "I'm Lutheran, don't go to church, but I believe in God and pray every night!" Then with a smile and a wave of his hand he jumped into his vehicle and was off down the road again. Glen did manage to give him one of our "Miles for Missions" brochures.

When the next service station came into view, we turned in to fill up the gas tank and to check the oil. "You can pay for the oil, but I'll give you the gas as a promo," the man said. Glen was delighted because the bill for the gas came to $37.00. And the same thing happened for us as we parked the rig and went to eat in a restaurant next door. After the meal, the waitress said, "My boyfriend who was sitting over there at that table paid for your meals."

Now that was really a surprise. We had noticed three young men sitting at a nearby table and we did not say a word to each other. We didn't think anything of it because locals know when there are strangers in town. They may have noticed that we got out of the tractor. Whatever the reason, we were blessed. God will take care of the details.

That night we met with an experience that was different from any of the many others we had encountered on the road. A forest fire was raging just two miles west of the highway. We watched as we were parked across the street from the airport for the night. Many airplanes and helicopters were carrying fire repellent materials from the airport to dump out over the fires. We slept peacefully, but probably many fire fighters and residents couldn't sleep.

During the forenoon, our new friends, Carlton and Nancy Baker, passed us. Many people waved and/or beeped their horns. Either they saw us the first time we drove through or read the *Yukon News* article. Whatever the reason, it is fun to wave.

The next morning the plastic covers on our tractor seats were covered with a film of ash from the fires. Because of the smoke from the forest fire hanging over the city, the sun did not shine that morning. The smoke was everywhere! We got to our destination, Johnson's Crossing, at five o'clock that evening. I told Glen I was the happiest woman in the camp because I caught up on laundry. It doesn't take much to make me happy.

We were glad to find a good Chinese restaurant in the Indian village of Teslin. It was just what we needed in meat, rice, and vegetables. After the meal, when we opened the fortune cookies, Glen's read: "Now is the time to try something new." My inscription read: "You are going to have a very comfortable old age," which amused us because of the assurance that God has plans for each one of His children as given in Jeremiah 29:11-13. They are of much greater significance than corny inscriptions in fortune cookies.

During the next few days, we encountered several steep inclines on the road and were amazed and pleased how the old John Deere conquered those hills. On one of the very long inclines, I wished someone could have recorded the sounds of the tractor's laboring and watched as it steadily climbed to the top with the trailer on its drawbar. These 1950 John Deere Model A tractors were built from very simple designs and are easy to work on. Dandelion had no speedometer, odometer, gas gauge, or power steering. Neither did our homemade tractor cab have air conditioning, heater, or windshield wipers like the modern machines have. We did have a heater available, but had no need to hook it up. We were, however, modern with our comfortable air-ride seats!

On August 19th, we pulled in at the last camping spot at Walker's Continental Divide and had a hearty breakfast in their restaurant the next morning. At this juncture, the waters divide into rivers that flow into the Arctic Ocean through the Mackenzie River system on the one side and those that drain into the Pacific Ocean via the Yukon River system on the other side. The weather was already turning cool enough that we had to wear several shirts and sweaters to cope with the lower temperatures.

We got into another construction area that was ten or twelve miles long. It was the watered down muddy mess again, and it "decorated" our mirrors and windows in a royal way. A few miles after we were out of that mess, we saw a sign labeled "Big Creek Day Camp." We decided here was our opportunity to wash the mud off.

To our pleasant surprise, as we turned into the campgrounds, we saw a group of Amish people from Kidron, Ohio standing by their RV waiting for us. Driver John Burdge, Abe and Anna Hochstetler and four children, as well as two friends were ready to welcome us. These people had been traveling for five weeks in Alaska and had been determined to find the "Miles for Missions" rig and travelers. They were overjoyed at the opportunity to meet us.

Back in the construction area, Abe had asked the flagger if a John Deere tractor had gone through there recently. She answered, "Yes, about twenty minutes ago," so then he was sure he would catch up with us.

Glen drove the rig down to the water and the fellows splashed water over the rig to clean off the mud, which made a great improvement, to say the least. As we pondered the events of the day, we again realized the providence of God, how He sends the right people along at the right time and right place. If the tractor had not been so muddy, we would not have driven to the Big Creek Day Camp where the Hochstetlers were waiting, and we would have missed meeting home-town people who helped with the cleaning and left us with a gift of smoked salmon.

We encountered steep hills on the way to Watson Lake where we stopped to eat our meal for the day. On we putted to Iron Creek for a long relaxing afternoon and evening which included a walk to the lake.

I served as the communication link between us and our church family. On this morning, before we left Green Valley RV Park, I took time off before hitting the road to check with our communications. This was a good time to call in our Internet update as well as check in with our children because of the three-hour time difference. How refreshing and encouraging it was to talk to all of them. We also received seven e-mail messages that our faithful friend, Dave Christner, read to us. I called Dave each Monday, Wednesday and Friday. He then relayed the message to Bart Winegar, who published it on the Internet web page.

On August 22nd we got an early start to cross a long stretch of construction on the highway. The volume of traffic was low, making it much easier for us to negotiate the rough places and the mud produced by the heavy earth-moving equipment. That day we traveled 96 miles and had to pay $.78.9 a liter (a little more than a quart) for gasoline—the highest price for fuel for the whole trip. Because of the approaching end to the tourist season, a marked decrease in traffic was very evident.

After driving 96 miles, we reached our destination—Laird Hot Springs Provincial Park. As Glen maneuvered the tractor and trailer past the many RV's in this popular place, a van followed fairly closely. Deciding that the people wanted to talk, he stopped and the woman in the van rolled down her window to tell us that they were from Magnolia, Ohio, and that she was raised in Wayne County. Small world!

Earl and Hazel Slutz were also on their way home from Alaska and had read about us in the *Dalton Gazette* and in the Anchorage newspaper. They were delighted to meet us. She was originally a Gerber from the Dalton area. They invited us to a picnic supper that evening and again to a camp-stove breakfast of eggs, home fries, ham, and coffee. As we parted, it seemed as though we had been friends for years.

At that same park, we met a couple with an unusual lifestyle. He is a retired Pan Am Airlines pilot. Eight months of the year they live on a houseboat in the Fiji Islands. During the summer months, they live in an RV, travel around the country, and visit their daughters who live in Alaska and California.

From that camp on, our route took us through some real mountainous traveling. Part of that phase of the trip took us around Muncho Lake, with truly magnificent scenery. We were glad to get to the Poplars Campground for the night. Since it was Sunday, the gas pumps and café were closed. Many campers were at this very neat place and paid the fees on Monday morning.

Then we faced climbing the road up Summit Lake Peak. With an elevation of 4,250 feet, it is the highest point on the Alaska Highway. Following that climb, we had to tackle Steamboat Mountain, with an elevation of 3,500 feet. Grinding along in fifth gear made for slower traveling on the putt putt as it labored faithfully up the steep grades.

Of course, what goes up must also come down, as the old saying goes. Driving downhill was every bit as challenging as climbing. We were thankful for the electric brakes on the trailer, which Glen could control from the tractor and added to the safety in the brake system of the rig. Having fewer vehicles on the highway and the road surface conditions good made Glen's job much easier. We were mountaineers for eight hours that day.

The night was spent in a campground somewhere in the midst of Steamboat Mountain. It is managed by a young family. We were again thankful for the Turbo heater that Jeff Hart had loaned us.

We went through Fort Nelson and on to Prophet River Services. While Glen was filling the gas tank on the tractor, I was inside the service station/restaurant combination. Several men asked me about the tractor and then said to the cashier, "We're paying for that gas. Anyone who has that kind of courage should have free gas!"

The men were geologists living and working on an oil project. British Columbia is rich in oil. A bit later the cashier told us to help ourselves to the buffet. "It's on the house!" We parked our rig there for a night of peaceful sleep while hearing the patter of rain.

There was a great deal of tedious traveling involved on the long, lonely parts of our route. This excerpt from my journal speaks of that: "We ate breakfast and started out on the Alaska Highway at 9:30. This is the only road! You cannot get lost or on the wrong road here. I begged Glen to write in the journal for today. I said he needs to put down his personal thoughts. He caught on and said, 'Just because nothing special has happened, you want me to do the writing!'"

There is so much loose gravel on the road. There must be thousands of "Loose Gravel" signs along the road in Alaska and Canada. When we were moving along at 13 miles per hour and I saw a little orange sign way in the distance, I knew what that sign would say. Those and the "No Litter" signs were by far the most predominant signs along the Highway. The big trucks and RVs really zoomed through the gravel making the dust and stones fly. But I kept reminding myself that the conditions could only get better.

After our overnight at Sikanni Chief Park (August 27th), we left and soon faced one of the toughest challenges of this leg of the journey. Climbing up the nine percent incline on the highway made the old John Deere hunker down in fifth gear and Glen finally had to shift into fourth because the clutch began to slip. The incline took us around a curve without shoulders on which to pull off. There were also deep crevices washed out along the right side of the road, so there was nothing we could do but chug along in fourth gear until we finally got to the top. Mercifully, a litter barrel turnoff provided a place where Glen was able to stop and adjust the tractor clutch so that it would run much better.

As we finally got out of those mountains, the traveling became much smoother and faster. The scenery changed from all pine trees to poplars and a variety of bushes. Farms began to appear along the way, with horses and cows grazing in pasturelands in this part of British Columbia.

Shepherd's Inn was the last overnight campsite on the Alaska Highway. While there, we met Emanuel Erb, formerly from Holmes County, Ohio, but now a confirmed Canadian who said he and his family love living in British Columbia. That night we needed the turbo heater in the trailer. Night was coming early again, at nine o'clock.

I could not resist buying a souvenir at the Inn. It consisted of an inch and a half square block of wood with the instructions: *"1. Place block on floor. 2. Walk around it twice. 3. Sit down. Relax! You have just walked around the block twice!"*

We got to the Alshart RV Park in Dawson Creek at 3:30, thankful to find a place to park and to rest in our trailer. The owner gave us a certificate that reads, "This is to certify that Glen and Betty Martin have successfully negotiated the many treacherous miles of the Alaska Highway, are and shall always be capable of anything Mother Nature and/or Murphy's law will throw at them." Now that is an exaggeration, but it was fun receiving it anyway.

On August 28th we came to the end of the official Alaska Highway. We had camped 38 times on the highway on this round trip. But as we traveled on, we began encountering more hills, several of them quite steep. Around the Fort St. John area, heavy traffic slowed us down, as well as road maintenance work where new coats of blacktop were being applied. Waiting periods became "trying periods" for us, sometimes as long as twenty minutes a stop, after which we had to wait until all of the vehicles passed us (seemed like as many as a hundred) before Glen could start the tractor up again.

We received many gifts of free gasoline, lodging, and food, but perhaps the most novel of all the gifts came at a waiting period on the road. A young man strolled over to the tractor and handed us two cans of orange soda pop. He told us that he was from North Pole, Alaska, had seen us on TV Channel 4, and was heading south to go to college in Virginia.

Leaving Dawson Creek, we anticipated being with the Terry and Marcy Balisky family overnight. As we putt-putted our way into Alberta on the Emerson Trail, three separate men, each in a pickup truck, stopped us. First, Daniel Loberg recognized us as we passed his farm and drove out to meet us. He had helped work on the tractor the previous month on our way north. The second man invited us to his church at Crooked Creek for the next day (Sunday). The third man, Dave Schmidt, was plowing his field when he noticed the John Deere chugging by. He said he felt that the Lord wanted him to catch up with us to encourage us on our mission. He also told us of a man who had committed his life to the Lord that very morning, which was especially good news for us to hear.

Since Crooked Creek was too far out of the way for us to attend on Sunday morning, we went with Terry and Marcy to McLaurin Baptist Church instead. Neighbors Ed and Irene Wiebe on the Emerson Trail invited us to their home for supper. Later, Dave and Ev Schmidt and Doris Fast came to hear all about the travels of the Ohio couple, which made for fond memories for all of us.

The next morning we left for Grand Prairie, where we put the tractor into a dealer's shop. The wear and tear of the trip was showing on Dandelion. The crew at the Peace Farm Power Shop was glad to see the John Deere and us again. On the trip north they had replaced the grease seal on the right rear tractor axle. This time they replaced the seal on the left axle, as well as reversing the rear tires because they were wearing faster on the curb side than on the other one.

When the work was completed, Arnie Romaniuk, one of the employees, said that he wanted to clean off the tractor with the pressure washer, making the tractor shine again. We appreciated his servant's attitude so much.

We left Grand Prairie to find Smoky River Provincial Campground. Before we could cover the 20 miles, the sun set and we were half an hour away from the camp. We knew it wasn't safe to be on the busy road after dark. The only thing to do was stop at a residence and trust God for a favor. We did stop at a home where there was sufficient area to turn around. A man with a kind countenance came outside. He said he had heard of us and after learning of our predicament, offered to follow us. With his car lights flashing, he followed us to the camp entrance, turned around and went home. It seemed as though an angel had guarded us. We don't even know his name.

The previous month, we had met Neil Holmes and his wife in the Crooked Creek area. Neil had invited us to stop by when we came through again, which we did. But no one was home, so after leaving a note, we continued on toward Valleyview. When we reached Valleyview, we called Art and May Joy Adolphson. Leaving their fieldwork, our new friends joined us in a nearby restaurant to catch up on the latest travel news. It was refreshing again to meet this dedicated couple who had been giving out the Jesus film in northern Alaska.

Driving along on Route 43 toward Whitecourt the next day, Glen noticed that the alternator was not charging properly. After stopping to fill up with gas, he had a hard time starting the tractor again. Asking about a camping site, we decided on the Lions Campground at the east end of the city. The camp had good accommodations. Also, the manager lived right at the camp, which was to come in handy for us later on.

Our next stopping place was to be with Syd and Nettie Spiker near Morinville. When Glen called to tell them of our plans, the phone only rang once and Syd answered energetically, "Glen! Is that you?"

That was such a surprise to Glen that he burst out laughing. He talked with Syd awhile and then described the alternator problem. They decided that a battery charger would be helpful. The camp manager provided one for us and Glen hooked it up to the battery for the night.

In the morning, the Spikers called to check on the situation. Although Glen was able to start the tractor engine, the alternator still was not working. They agreed that we would start down the road and the Spikers were to meet us at noon with a new alternator and tools to replace the old one. By noon the Spikers' red truck had come, and in a short time the new alternator was in place right there in a service station parking lot.

The Spikers returned to their work only an hour away. We went our usual speed, stopped at the Mayerthorpe John Deere dealer's place, then journeyed to the Spiker residence. Their home had become almost like a home away from home because of their gracious hospitality, both as we were going north and now on the return trip toward home. We put the tractor into the Spiker Equipment Shop for a good "going over". The mechanics changed the oil and the filter and checked all of the screws and bolts on the cab, some of which had come loose from the vibration. They also inspected the gas line and filter for sediment. The old John Deere was soon smiling again and ready to go.

For weeks Glen was wondering where he could get his hair cut. It turned out that this was the day. Syd suggested a barber who had been in the business for 35 years. The same day we went to the Wal-Mart for supplies. In the evening, the Spikers invited friends over again for a picnic. Several were people whom we had met two months earlier, as well as some new people. Even though the evening was chilly, we pulled our lawn chairs close to the fire and had a good time of fellowship and sharing.

That night as I sat in the Spikers' shop office writing in my journal, I wrote, "As I am writing, I can hear a radio playing very softly. I can barely hear it, but two lines of a song are coming through as if they were intended just for me: *'All I have needed, Thy hand hath provided. Great is Thy faithfulness, Lord, unto me.'* Now I am straining to hear more music, but I can hear nothing. Thank you, Lord, for reminding me how much You care!"

Sunday morning we worshiped with the people at the Cornerstone Pentecostal Church in St. Albert with the Spikers. We participated in the service by speaking to the congregation and taking part in the communion supper with the body of believers. We enjoyed the warm spirit that we sensed among the leaders and members of the congregation.

We had decided to take a different route out of Alberta to continue our trip toward home. Syd and Nettie were a great help in mapping out a route through southern Alberta and eventually into Montana. It was a little sad saying "good-bye" to these friends, but we believe we will see them again since they enjoy traveling.

I remembered asking the Lord to send campers so we could visit at another site. He answered that prayer. Tonight I prayed the same request and, thankfully, He heard me again. We were in our trailer in Camrose when a van and camper stopped by our rig. We had a pleasant visit with Nels and Marion Loberg, retired missionaries after 40 years in the country of Bolivia, South America. It was special for us to meet this couple who had spent so many years abroad, but were not resting on their laurels. They were still in ministry, selling Christian books and greeting cards. The Lobergs took us to their home there in Camrose to select some books to read along the way. We chose *One Bright Shining Path,* by Terry Whaline and Chis Woehr, and *Rwanda, a Walk Through Darkness Into Light,* by Carl Lawrence.

On September 8th we had to drive more miles than usual—112. It was more difficult to find a camping area than on the Alaskan Highway. There was not even one rest area with public restrooms along Route 56. Guess they didn't plan for any slow-moving vehicles to pass that way. Finally, we came to a *very* steep eight percent grade into the town of Drumheller. We looked in the *Pentecostal Church Directory* someone had given us way back in June and found there was a church in this town. A telephone call brought the pastor to our aid and he directed us to his church for electrical hook-up.

Continuing on with our journey toward home, we got onto the Trans

Canadian Highway south of the small town of Hussar. That highway is a divided highway with a good right shoulder. There was not much traffic and the skies were overcast, so we did not have the glare of bright sunshine with which to contend on that 9th day of September. We came to the small town of Bassano, which had a John Deere dealership, so Glen stopped there briefly. As always, the workers at the shop were simply amazed that the old "two-popper" Dandelion was able to keep faithfully putt-putting along the many miles the way it did. Our hubodometer showed 6,648 miles that evening.

We were blessed to find an extra nice campsite just off the Trans Canadian Highway between the towns of Brooks and Tilley. It was appropriately named Tillebrook. Glen had planned to stop in Tilley for gas in the morning. Just as we were ready to leave, the grounds manager came by to see the rig. Glen mentioned that we planned to go to Tilley for gas, but the manager informed us there is no gas station in that small town and that we would need to go back north a mile for the nearest station. This was another example of the Lord providing the right person at the right place at the right time to avoid our running out of fuel.

We had to drive through the cities of Radcliffe and Medicine Hat, which stretched for miles along the Trans Canadian Highway. Driving during the rush hours was a real challenge for Glen. The maps showed a camping site called Cypress Hills. We had no alternative but to putt-putt into that forsaken place. The facilities were just the opposite from the previous night—no electric hook-up and no water. It was weedy and cluttered.

September 11th was our last day in Canada. That morning we stopped at a gas station where we had asked for directions to an overnight camp the evening before. After filling the tractor with fuel and ordering some coffee, we had only $2.16 in Canadian money left in change. We decided to just keep it. We had enjoyed our journey through the pleasant miles of Canada. Now we had 45 miles to Montana.

Canada and its friendly people left memories and thoughts of endearment forever on our hearts. The wild, rugged beauty of some of its mountain country, the vast open spaces of its prairies, the fertile farmlands, and honest sincerity of its hospitable citizens made traveling in Canada a cherished experience, one that we will never forget. My journal is filled with names and references to people, in most cases complete strangers, who went out of their way to welcome us along the way and to help assure us success in our venture. What a beautiful gift from God this was!

Eleven

*"Do not withhold your mercy from me, O Lord;
may your love and your truth always protect me."* Psalm 40:11

Montana ∿

September 11th

HELLO USA!" WE WERE FINALLY BACK IN THE STATES! Before officially entering back into the USA, we had to stop at the customs house in Wild Horse, Montana. A sign was posted: "STOP. PLEASE STAY IN VEHICLE." Stepping out of his office, the official came up to the tractor and said to Glen, "Hey, park your rig back there on the parking lot and come into my office. We can't hear to talk with that two-popper going like that!"

So we followed him into his station where he asked us a few of the questions usually asked at such customs posts. When Glen answered "Yes" to the man's question of "Are you an American?" the officer looked at him and said, "How can you prove it?"

"We were both born in Ohio," Glen answered.

The smiling officer then said, "Well, that'll do it every time!"

Then he told us how he used to crank an old handstarter John Deere when he was a boy, still so young that he could barely handle the crank wheel. The officer seemed to enjoy seeing Dandelion and us. Before we left, Glen took a picture of the man standing beside the tractor, hugely pleased with the opportunity.

He said to us as we left, "Now please be careful as you drive along, because there is no speed limit in Montana. People have a habit of doing a lot of drinking on weekends and drive too fast." Then one of the first signs we saw along Highway 233 was "Car speed limit: Reasonable and Prudent."

A sad scene met our eyes as we drove on through Montana. There were many white crosses along the way where traffic accidents had taken the lives of people. At one place we saw five crosses and at another seven, marking where lives had been lost.

Traveling from that entry point on the lonely part of the road toward Havre, we met with the problem that every motorist or trucker dreads —we ran out of gas! Fortunately, we had a nine-gallon spare tank mounted on the tongue of the trailer and it got us to the next service station at 5:30 that evening in Havre. This continued to be lonely country, with mailboxes at the ends of lanes so long that one could not see the farm buildings to which they belonged.

Now we were back to handling U.S. money again and talking about miles instead of Canadian kilometers. I wonder how many hundreds of times I had to get my little calculator out of my purse to multiply kilometers x .62 to get the reading in miles.

We left Havre at 8:45 a.m. and soon noticed a John Deere dealer along the way. Stopping there, Glen went in to talk with the dealer. He told Glen that business was naturally slow because of the fall season, but the countryside was very dry because of lack of rain. Farmers were unable to plow or plant their fall crops because of the parched ground. Speaking of John Deere dealerships, at one place the men's restroom had "John" on the door and "Deere" on the women's door. At another stop they were labeled "Bucks" and "Does".

As we rode along day after day, unable to talk with each other because of the tractor noise, we tried to notice the unusual and amusing sights along the way. One such sight was cattle dashing away from the edge of the pasture fields when they heard the rig coming by. One day two horses galloped away as fast as they could up over a steep hill and then turned, stopping to stand and stare at us in wonder and bewilderment, almost as if to say, "Hey, how can you do this to us?" We also saw some ducks feeding and meandering around a pond. When we approached, some flew away, while others nonchalantly kept paddling along in the water as though nothing could disturb them from their good time swimming.

On our journey today an old car painted lemon yellow whizzed by; then later one painted lavender passed us on the highway. Since the town of Chinook lay just up the road, we decided to stop for a short while. Several men came along to us and asked if we would park the rig among a number of their antique cars and tractors for their special "Western Days" festival that was in progress. I guess the yellow and lavender cars were part of that affair, too. Because of time limits we had to politely refuse. We needed to keep pressing on to reach our destination for the evening.

Before we left for Alaska, Edgar Raber, a fellow member of our home church, said that if we came home through Montana, he would fly out to visit his friend, Tim Bartholomew, who lives in Kalispell, Montana. Then they would try to meet us somewhere out there. Edgar did just that. He flew to Spokane; then he and Bartholomew drove 350 miles to catch up with us on our tractor on Route 2, east of Harlem. To our delight, the two men were wearing "Miles for Missions" T-shirts as they climbed out of their truck to meet us. What a happy meeting this was! After 90 minutes of hugging, laughing, sharing accounts of the trip, and praying together, we parted again. Tim and Edgar retraced the 350 miles back to Kalispell, while Glen pulled the throttle back on old Dandelion and we continued putt-putting eastward.

That night we camped at the town of Malta after a drive of 89 miles. "Trains, trains, trains," I wrote in my journal. "All night long the trains clattered over the big railroad bridge across the Milk River right behind our camper. There must have been three or four speeding across every hour. In spite of the noise we did get a pretty good rest." This surely was a big contrast for us after the long, silent expanses of the Canadian prairies and the Yukon where only roads and highways cut across the countryside.

The drive to Glasgow along the Milk River that day was the hottest day of our trip thus far. The temperature climbed to 92 degrees Fahrenheit. The hours crawled slowly along with only an occasional welcome breeze coming through the tractor cab as we passed along the vast sweep of the open Montana fields and the wide, overarching sky.

The opportunities to witness for the Lord, to our faith and reasons for our trip came in all kinds of different places and to different people. The next day as we were leaving the campground at Malta, a lady news reporter stopped us and requested an interview. So we agreed to meet in a nearby restaurant. During the breakfast she asked a long list of questions and when the waitress brought the bill, the reporter paid for the food. Then the lady wanted to share some issues in her own family situation. We pray that the seed that was sown for the Lord in her heart will bear fruit in her.

Many restaurants in Montana have gambling devices on the premises as part of their business. An old man at that early hour on a Monday morning was already playing the machines, a sad contrast to the joy we feel in witnessing for our Saviour in whom we trust and in whom alone there is real security.

As we drove, we could easily read the signs. One sign had these words: "Prepare for Jesus' Coming." This suggestion was both different and wonderful.

Before starting out on another new day, I called in the update. Dave Christner said we would have a three-way conversation. I was delighted to hear the voice of Duane Galbraith, our youth pastor, who shared words of encouragement and prayed with me. It was an inspirational way to start the day. Even the weather was perfect!

That day we drove from Glasgow to Wolf Point, east on Route 2, and then south on Route 13 to the village of Circle where we camped for the night at a small RV facility. The next morning we had a hard time getting started for the road because of visitors wanting to talk. A John Deere dealer came along and told a widower who was talking with us to take us to breakfast at the restaurant across the way. He would pay for it all. Mission accomplished.

Orrville Quick, from Circle, persuaded us to stop for an interview with Cindy Mullet from Glendive. He arranged the time and place, which we found without difficulty. It was hot as we sat in our trailer to answer her questions. Cindy was pleasant and easy to converse with. A copy of her newspaper article was sent to us. We concluded that Cindy is a good and truthful reporter.

Because of the late start, we did not get on the road until the day was already quite hot. Finally arriving in the town of Wibaux (pronounced wee' bow), while stopping to fill up with gasoline, we met a young fellow who said that he was a Christian and wanted to pay for our overnight stay in a nearby Motel 8. What a nice change that was! That evening we watched the first television newscast since we had left Ohio for Alaska. We decided there was not much news worth watching and did not feel we had missed much during those months. Looking back to that morning, I admitted to myself that I had been disappointed because of the late start; but now I saw the Lord's hand in it. Had we not been delayed, we would have missed the generous Christian fellow who provided us the overnight in the motel! And Kevin and Traci Anderson would have missed the blessing of sharing.

After a good night's rest, we awoke to greet the dawn of September 16th. Walking toward the rig, we noticed a truck camper from Minnesota stopping by Dandelion. We met the Stan Sandmans and young grandson Micah with whom we visited awhile and learned that he was a John Deere enthusiast. Imagine Glen's surprise when the man told him that he has 35 old John Deere tractors that he is restoring. Several months previously, the Sandmans had read about the "Miles for Missions" venture in the *Green Magazine*. When they saw the rig parked by the motel, they turned in from the highway to meet us.

When we came into the town of Baker, we immediately recognized it as an oil town. All the businesses seemed to be oil related. The gas station attendant complained that there were six bars in town and only one grocery store. There were also no fast food eating places in Baker. The closest large discount store, like a Wal-Mart, was 81 miles away.

The Dakotas ∿

September 16th

At 2:20 that afternoon we saw the sign that welcomed us into North Dakota and the small village of Marmarth. The village got its name, we were told, by having been named after two sisters: Mary and Martha. Route 12 now took us through the southwestern corner of North Dakota.

Seven miles before we got to Bowman, our destination for the day, a woman reporter stopped us and arranged for an interview with her and her husband in town. Half an hour later we arrived in Bowman, where the reporters were waiting. We saw the first fields of corn and sunflowers in North Dakota. That evening we camped on the eastern end of town, with only three other camper units at that site.

The next night (September 17th) we slept at the Waterhole Campground in Lemmon. In the morning we wanted to be up at 6:30 and on our way; but at that hour driving straight into the sunrise, we had a difficult time seeing to drive because the sunlight reflected so severely from the plexiglass of our cab. So we actually had to wait until the sun had risen higher in the sky before getting out on the road again. For most of the 102 miles that day, we were driving through the Standing Rock Indian Reservation.

The following night we slept at the Indian View Campground, near Mobridge, South Dakota, along with many other campers and millions of mosquitoes. We enjoyed the spectacular sunset that evening and the sweeping beauty of the vast open western skies. There was a sense of achievement as we entered South Dakota. Now there were only three states left to travel through before we got to Ohio.

In South Dakota we traveled along Route 12 until we came to Aberdeen, where we had a delightful reunion with Glen's cousins, the Zieglers, with whom we had stayed on our way north. They had just returned from Iowa the night before and drove out to meet us. They returned home and we got to their place two hours later. Again, we marveled at the beauty of the clouds.

After worshiping with them at the Aberdeen United Methodist Church, we had lunch with James and Kathlyn Ziegler, Dale Ziegler, and Beverly and Ray Mack, Dale's daughter and son-in-law.

Even though the weather would have been perfect for traveling, we chose to visit with our relatives and with John Deere enthusiast, 79-year-old John Pulfrey. While the men were talking "green machine" stuff, I enjoyed getting to know John's 83-year-old sister Lourene, who had taught school for thirty years and had also worked for several years in the Pentagon.

Monday morning Glen and James did check-up maintenance on the tractor. I caught up with laundry, called in the Internet update, and wrote cards. Kathlyn served us a good meal again and at 12:30 the putt-putt sound rang through the air and we were off for another stretch of driving.

We camped at Redford and in the morning we drove a short distance to a restaurant. The instant we opened the door, an older man exclaimed, "We were just talking about you when you drove in! Your pictures and story are in the *"Aberdeen American Newspaper."* One of the men then gave us a copy of the paper. When we were finished eating, the waitress brought a copy of the article and asked for our autographs so she could put it on the bulletin board. Then she picked up the tab and said, "I'll take care of this!" Which, of course, was a blessing and a nice way for us to start the day.

Soon it was time to travel on. We saw God's plan at work again when we met a local man who directed us over a different route than we had planned because of construction.

We were in the middle of nowhere and had no idea where to find a campsite. Out in the country where we stopped for gas, a young lady had just come to start her work shift. She told of a camping spot 20 miles down the direction we were traveling. The weather and roads were in our favor and we made it there before dark.

In this area we were impressed with the small town of Woonsocket. The houses were neat, the lawns well kept, and the streets clean. The street signs were red with white lettering, giving it the look of a town of which its citizens were proud enough to keep it neat and attractive. So, roses to the residents of Woonsocket, South Dakota.

The weather turned cooler, which made the driving so much more pleasant for us. We drove to the town of Canistota, the town where the famous Ortman Chiropractic Clinic is located. Amish and others from many different states travel to this clinic for medical treatments. Since we had taken Henry B. and Mary Yoder from Charm, Ohio to this clinic several years ago, we thought it would be interesting to stop again. We met the Enos D. Hershbergers from Harmony, Minnesota, Crist C. Stutzman and the Dan D. Hershbergers from Canton, Minnesota, and Dan A. Hershberger from Knox County, Ohio. Each of these people have relatives living in our area in Ohio.

I met a very interesting couple from Iowa. After we chatted awhile, I asked the woman to write their names in my legal pad. Seeing that the writing was so neat, I asked if she used to be a schoolteacher. She smiled as she answered, "Yes." This dear woman, Verna Myers, is 92, has sharp understanding, and hears well. Her companion, Pearl, is 88.

He told us Verna has been his girlfriend for 66 years! What a wonderful story of long-lasting love. I very much enjoy talking to older people and gleaning the beautiful jewels of life in the past. I can always benefit from them and improve my own outlook on life.

We were ready to leave Canistota with the route directions written out by Norman so we could avoid a road under construction. He called them chicken scratches, but they were exactly what we needed. Norman had also found us a place to park the night before by a motel where we could plug in and relax without cost. That town is fortunate to have a handy man like Norman around.

In the town of Viborg a group of men came to see the tractor. They could hardly believe that we had driven that tractor to Alaska and had traveled 8,400 miles up to then. One old fellow looked at me with tears in his eyes and said, "Thank you for stopping in our town. I know the Lord is watching over you." It certainly is true—a good, sturdy tractor, friendly people along the way, and the Lord watching over us was indeed a winning combination for the "Miles for Missions" couple.

Iowa ⌒

Right after getting into Iowa, in the town of Hawarden, we ran into trouble with the flashing lights on the tractor. When we started out for the road in the morning the lights simply would not flash. Glen got a new flasher unit, but it still did not work until he took the tractor to an auto body shop which also did electrical repair work. After moving the ground cable, the flashers worked again. Our problem was solved. That day we did not get on the road again until 12:20, after lunch.

We headed for the Crossroad Motel at the junction of Highways 3 and 11. We were to meet Al and Faye (Hochstetler) Swartzentruber who live in Storm Lake. They are relatives of our friend Dave Christner. Al and Faye were formerly from Holmes County, Ohio. They had made arrangements with Dave to meet us. Then the large strobe light on top of the trailer quit working. Finally, just before dark, Glen called the Swartzentrubers, who came and followed us, with their car lights flashing to avoid motorists from coming suddenly upon our slow-moving rig in the dark and running into us. Usually we did not travel after dark, but that night we had to meet a schedule.

The kind motel owner donated a room for overnight to us. Before we settled down, Al and Faye walked with us to a nearby restaurant for refreshments and fellowship. Our circle of friends continued to grow wherever we went, with each person contributing uniquely in encouraging us on our mission. Early the next morning Glen was able to find the trouble and had the strobe working again before we left Iowa.

Along the route, we stopped in Hampton and Oelwein to visit people with whom we had made friends on the way through during the summer. Twice during the morning, as we drove on Route 3, a white panel truck passed us. These three words were painted on the back: "There Goes Martin". We liked that.

In the town of Cascade, we could not find a campground, so Glen asked at the police station where we could camp, and they permitted us to stay in the town park even though a sign at the entrance said that it was prohibited. He said he would notify the night security guard. We felt rather privileged with the special treatment.

Around 8:30, a car drove in beside our trailer. Glen went out to see who it was. The man said he had read about our venture just a couple of days earlier in the *Green Magazine* and now he saw the very tractor he read about. He was so excited because "nothing special ever happens in this little town of Cascade and now there is real news for the newspaper!" That John Deere enthusiast just could not "get over it." In the morning, a news reporter came for pictures and a story.

Eugene Bruhn of Miles, Iowa and Bert Shaw of Savanna, Illinois, were working on the road when they heard the unmistakable sound of the two-popper engine. They motioned Glen to stop. These men had seen us putt-putt through there on our way north several months before. They now wanted to know if we had actually made the trip to Alaska. They left a handful of butterscotch candies with us as they bade us good-bye.

Illinois ～

On the last day of September, we finally crossed the Mississippi River and at the end of the big bridge read the sign: "The People of Illinois Welcome You!" We were finally back in Illinois! I folded up the Iowa map. Now we could move along in Illinois. We anticipated stopping at the Land of Oz gas station and restaurant complex near Mt. Carroll. Rich and Carol Frey were still cheerfully serving the customers. We appreciated their thoughtfulness.

In the Woosung-Sterling area, a father and son stopped us on the road. To our pleasant surprise he introduced himself as Howard Landis. His wife, Erma (Keim) was formerly from my home area. They are both 77 years old and had read about us and our "Miles for Missions" trip in *The Budget*, a newspaper published in Sugarcreek, Ohio with Amish and Mennonite subscribers all over the Americas.

Sandwich was the next stopover area where we stayed with John, Roberta, Corey, and Noel Ressler. Six-year-old Noel loves to sing and has a good voice, so she, her mother, and I had our own "hymn sing" before she went to bed. Corey, who is ten, preferred to sit and listen to "man talk".

In July, Russell Lauderbach from the town of Watseka had given us his copy of the travel guide *Milepost* which was invaluable on our trip north. Now, as we approached that town, we were determined to give the copy back to Russell. When we stopped for gas in town, Glen called him. Russell and his wife Jean came to meet us. We had lunch and a good time of fellowship together before getting back on the road. Just a few miles out of town, a young man flagged us down to tell us that his parents had been to Alaska, too. It turned out to be the Lauderbachs' son.

We first met Brian Short, a Motel 8 manager, on June 8th on our way west. Today we were driving on that same road and Glen stopped to check if Brian was around. He was there, so we had an enjoyable time of visiting. The world could use lots of "Brians". He directed us away from a heavy construction area. We felt God had us stop there so we would be told. I had to think of "Our stops are ordered by God as much as our steps."

As we traveled east the next day we met with a lot of heavy rain. Coming into Indiana, we passed through the town of Goodland. We were amused with the sign near the end of town which read: "Our Name Says it All." A young man came up to the rig and said he had read about us and wanted to give a donation for our mission. He gave us all the money that he had in his pocket: $1.09. The Lord will bless any amount.

Near the small town of Wolcott, a family was out on the porch and all were waving to us. Our hearts were touched. We could feel their love.

In the town of Logansport, we hit the heaviest traffic of the whole trip. It was like stampeding horses in all four lanes. Finally, Glen had to pull off the road to allow the cars to go by; but then we could not break back into the flow of traffic again. We waited and waited for a lull in the stream of cars, but there was none! We hardly knew what to do when suddenly a family came out of a Pizza Hut along that part of the street. Coming up to us, they asked all about the "Miles for Missions" project. When we were finished visiting to our satisfaction, the couple stepped out into the traffic and motioned for us to bring the rig back onto the road. We were so grateful to that couple. It took us over an hour to get out of that heavy flow of traffic. Neither of us ever cares to go back to Logansport again, but we see God's plans in various ways every day. We praise Him for His faithfulness.

Charlie and Peg Thompson of Bluffton, Indiana rolled out the welcome mat for us on the night of October 4th. Their caring and sharing way of life makes it a pleasure to be with them. While there, we met a variety of people aged five to eighty. These included Paul Reiff, Roger Ploughe, Clara Schilling, Marvin Day, Kelly and Carl Thompson, Tammy Saalfrank and children Wayne and Elayne, as well as Charlie and Peg's granddaughters, Chelsea and Kendyl, and their mother. A lady reporter also stopped for pictures and a story.

Glen called his sister and husband and another couple who had expressed interest in seeing our rig and us. This morning, October 5th, they all came to the Thompsons to visit: LeRoy and Mabel (Glen's sister) Nisley, their friends Oscar and Ann Packer from Middlebury, Leroy and Pat Grabill from New Paris, and Mildred Knutti from our home area in Ohio. This was another highlight of our journey, as our circle of friends grew ever larger. We were blessed to know that they drove nearly 100 miles one way just to be with us.

We had not seen Mildred for 27 years, so it was special seeing her again. Our boys used to work for Knuttis selling plants in the spring of the year.

"Welcome to Ohio" ∽ _____

At eleven o'clock the next day, we saw the sign for which we were eagerly watching on Route 124: "Welcome to Ohio." We then moved our watches an hour ahead to be on the same time as our families at home. Traveling just south of Lima, we encountered heavy traffic again because of the rush hour.

Several times after we got back into the States, we noticed that the route signs on the maps did not correspond with the signs posted along the highways. This was very frustrating. On this day we got lost because of it. We were placing our confidence in the road signs but they were leading us southeast instead of east. Glen finally stopped and asked a man for directions and found that we were indeed heading the wrong way. Since darkness was fast approaching, we decided to accept the hospitality of the Larry Mizeks and parked by their house for the night.

Larry built a campfire in a cage-type container in their yard and we sat out by the fire and visited awhile before retiring for the night.

"This is our last night on this memorable trip," I wrote in my journal on October 7th. "We are in a motel room in Bellville, Ohio and the rain continues to fall! Our friends, Paul and Muriel Lang from Pataskala, wanted us to tell them when we got to this area, so we walked over to the motel office to call them. We made plans to meet them tomorrow to have breakfast together."

October 8th and a new day dawned, refreshed and important after all the rain. We were so grateful to have a pleasant day for completing our long journey. The Langs arrived soon after eight o'clock, and after the greetings and hugs we drove a few miles down the road to the Der Dutchman Restaurant for a hearty breakfast. To my surprise, looking up from the menu, I saw a group of my cousins there, too. They are from Holmes County. Meeting Oletha Troyer, Annetta Weaver, Lorene Gingerich, and Kenny Hamsher and wife Kathy added another special dimension to the morning for us.

The remaining 60 miles home consisted of short and steep hills. Glen had to do a lot of shifting down for the grades, but Dandelion kept performing well in spite of the different lay of the land. The farm fields had become smaller. The leaves showed the splendor of autumn colors—reds, oranges, yellows, and browns against the backdrop of hills. The valleys, still green by contrast, made the countryside an inspiration of beauty, a reminder to us of the abundance of God's creative art and handiwork.

We had been asked by Dave Christner to call the church an hour before our arrival time in Millersburg. When we stopped to use our cell phone, our longtime friend Rich Fath stopped by. He had been looking for us. At 2:15 PM we stopped in front of our home church, the Lighthouse Christian Fellowship. A number of friends were eagerly waiting with excited greetings, smiles, and hugs.

Twenty miles still waited for us on our final lap of the long road. Five miles from our home, we called the grandchildren who live next door and told them to listen for the putt-putting of the tractor.

As we neared our driveway, a neighbor and her daughters were waving; two grandsons came charging through the pasture, crawled under the electric fence, and beat their sisters to our yard. The four granddaughters ran down the long driveway towards the house, with the three-year-old losing her pink slippers three times. Finally the oldest sister picked up the shoes and carried them the rest of the way. The two-year-old brother was napping and the oldest one was still working, so they missed out on the excitement. In a few days we saw the rest of our Ohio children and grandchildren, but had to wait until Christmas to see the ones from Texas.

We were parked in our driveway only a few minutes when Emmet Shafer and his wife Nancy from Stanwood drove up. We did not know them. The couple had seen us drive through Mt. Hope, so they rushed home and made a neat sign on their computer to give to us to welcome us home. What a thoughtful gesture that was, and a fitting end to our journey.

How grateful we were to be back home again, how grateful for the grace of God that enabled us to have the courage to be obedient to the vision He gave us. How thankful we were for the Lord's safety, protection, and directions on each of the 126 days on the long road! There were 96 days of actual driving. The 30 days we were not on the road included visiting with new friends and relatives along the way or "down times" for tractor repairs and maintenance, and many Sundays when we had stopped to worship in various churches along the way. We got home with the very same rear tires on the tractor that we had when we started, after 9,500 miles. God had honored our vision, our faith, our perseverance, and our compassion for the furthering of the Gospel of His great and eternal kingdom.

Conclusion ⌒ ————————————————————

By Les Troyer

Christian missions means miracles. It means rising above the inertia, the indifference to God's Holy Word by the lukewarm church, the hatred and opposition of Satan and the distracting forces of the world. It means scaling the cultural barriers of different people and societies. It means learning and mastering difficult languages. It means never faltering nor flinching in the face of seemingly insurmountable odds (Acts 20:22-24). It may mean driving an antique tractor all the way to Alaska and back to catch the attention of people for world missions.

Missions demands men and women willing to move out of their own comfort zones and out into the rough and tough byways of the world. It takes men and women filled with the Holy Spirit who are like a pure riverbed through which flows the power of God to do His work among people who have never heard the Gospel. And as these riverbed channels are filled, the Holy Spirit can do the miracle of missions through those who have obeyed His calling. Glen and Betty Martin are two such people whom God has called—and blessed!

Afterglow

"... Paul had a vision of a man of Macedonia standing and begging him, " 'Come over to Macedonia and help us.' After Paul had seen the vison, we got ready at once to leave for Macedonia, concluding that God had called us to preach the gospel to them." Acts 16:9-10

FTER WE LEFT TOK, ALASKA ON AUGUST 12th, we kept thinking about the pleading voice of Roy David, the man from the Tetlin Reservation. He had asked us to come to his village to teach about Jesus. His family members were the only Christians. We had to decline his request because the weather was turning cold earlier than usual in Alaska.

When Glen described the situation to our pastor, he responded with, "We must go and answer that Macedonian call."

It was decided that a team of three men from our church would go, befriend the First Nation people, and do whatever ministry the Lord would direct. So, after much praying and planning, Glen, John Strasser, and Youth Pastor Duane Galbraith left for Alaska (by plane this time) on June 28, 1999.

At 11:30 that night they arrived in the airport in Anchorage. An hour later the taxi in which they rode stopped at the hostel where they would sleep. Here the men were introduced to the land of the midnight sun where it was light as day all night. To say it was difficult to sleep is putting it mildly.

The next method of travel was a shuttle bus, which came at 9:00 AM and took them to Fairbanks by 5:45 PM. Our friend, Dick Olson from KJNP, came to meet them in the van, which KJNP loaned to the men to use while in Alaska. That same night, Dick interviewed John, Duane, and Glen on a radio program. Three tired men were so grateful for the sleeping facilities at KJNP that night.

Gen Nelson, president of KJNP, Dick and Bev Olson, and staff personnel were so kind and helpful in many ways. They will always be part of our best memories of the tractor trip as well as the trip described in this chapter.

Roy David's wife, Cora, had told Glen that the men would need to take their own food because there is no grocery store in Tetlin. A trip to Sam's Wholesale in Fairbanks on Wednesday was next on the agenda. It would have been interesting to watch three men buy several days' supply of food. Besides the mixed dried fruits and an assortment of canned items including peaches and sardines (which only Glen enjoyed), they brought two large bags of colorful tortillas and a big jar of salsa. After the canned foods were gone, they had chips and salsa for brunch, then salsa and chips later in the day.

It was around 200 miles from Fairbanks to Tok. Original plans were to get from Tok to Tetlin on a boat, but Roy informed them in a telephone conversation that a boat was not available. Fortunately, there was a small airport in Tok where bush pilots were on hand. So, Plan B was activated and the three courageous men climbed aboard a small plane after they had loaded up a fair amount of luggage. The plane was so filled that when it landed, the tail hit the runway before the front wheels. Thankful for a safe trip, the men climbed out, unloaded, and looked around for Roy David.

But Roy was not around. Through a misunderstanding, he thought the men would arrive the next morning. They had to communicate with one of the men to ask how the luggage could be taken to Roy's house. He just pointed at a pickup truck as he said, "That's a village truck. Use it." So Duane jumped in, but the clutch didn't work, so he turned on the key and it lurched forward and kept moving. The luggage was piled on the truck and taken to Roy's place.

By this time John, Glen, and Duane felt sort of "let down", but decided to find the house of Evelyn Paul, Roy's niece. They succeeded in finding her. She suggested they go back to Roy's home and wait for him. There was a period of just plain waiting until Roy finally returned in the evening.

Roy David is a man who is concerned about his people. As they were visiting in Roy's home, he related what happened last August when he made the first contact with us on the tractor trip.

He sensed a moving from God to go out to the Alaska Highway where he would meet some Christian people to fellowship with for a short time. He was to ask those people to come to Tetlin to teach the Word. He invited his niece Evelyn and her children to go along. When Evelyn asked whom he would meet, he could only answer, "I don't know, but God told me to go."

They drove out over a very rough road to get to Tok. When he saw our rig parked in a business parking lot, he said, "There they are!" After talking with us and understanding why we couldn't go with him at that time, he wept as we putted down the road. He felt we would return someday.

Now here sat Glen, John, and Duane in answer to his request.

That same night after 9 o'clock (who goes to bed when it stays light?) Roy, Cora, and Evelyn invited adults in to be ministered to. Many came and wept as Duane, John, and Glen prayed and asked God to deliver them from generational sins. They went to bed at midnight with great anticipation of what might happen on Thursday.

Thursday came around, but the people didn't come around. Three discouraged men were not aware that most everyone had gone fishing . . . not for a few hours, but all day! Time was not wasted, though, for the Ohioans. After munching on chips and salsa they had seasons of prayer, asking God to allow them to reach the people in the village. There was a request for protection. It was an unusual day without the locals around.

Friday morning came and with it a stirring of the people. Roy explained that during Thursday night, a man with a gun was roaming the village seeking revenge in some situation. You will recall that they had prayed for protection. People called by telephone to ask the men to come to their houses to pray. Duane went to a number of homes while John and Glen went to others. It was a blessed day of ministry.

Friday afternoon three visitors came. Seeing that they were Americans, the men went to meet them. Cristina Welker, the young woman, was the schoolteacher at Tetlin last year and will be back for another year of teaching. She had brought her parents to see the village and school. They were from Cincinnati, Ohio.

It was of special significance that they met at this time. The team was scheduled to fly out the next day. They had brought toys and games to give to the children, but hesitated to give them because there were more children than toys and the end result wouldn't be good. Now it was decided to give the toys to the teacher and she could pass them out as rewards during the school year.

Also, the men wondered where a team of workers could stay if and when they came to the village for further ministry. Cristina said they could stay in the school where there would be suitable accommodations. She is in full charge of the school building.

Prayers of thanksgiving were on the men's hearts as they thought of God's timing. That day they also met the village Chief. He gave them a warm welcome and promised to give assistance for a church building.

Saturday morning's schedule was for departure time at 8:00 AM, but it was too windy for the small airplane. The Tetlin population was headed for Tok for ball games and fireworks. Because of this annual July 4th celebration, few people were left in town. In the afternoon, around 5:00, the airplane came. The pilot said, "I don't want as heavy a load as the last time. I'll take you (Duane) and you (John) and your luggage." They left at 5:45 for the ten-minute flight. As they landed, they noticed a cloud of smoke in the distance. Meanwhile, as Glen was standing back in Tetlin, a heavy rain moved in. He pushed his luggage under a nearby truck that was locked and crawled into another truck with the owner.

When the plane came, the pilot was nervous as he said, "Hurry, we've got to rush out because of forest fire smoke!" In went the luggage and Glen. Then two women said they wanted to go, too. "Hurry!" They were off and just a minute later, the smoke was so thick the pilot couldn't see any land. You can be sure that Glen prayed. He asked God to give the pilot more wisdom than he'd ever had. They were lost and had to fly by instructions from the tower in Tok. They had to circumnavigate a mountain range. Later, Glen found out there was another airplane in the same area with which they could have collided. After at least half an hour, they landed exactly right on the Tok airstrip. The pilot remarked, "I'll never fly in smoke again!"

Now the men could take their belongings to the KJNP van that was parked at the airport. They looked forward to being with their North Pole friends, but they couldn't leave just yet because someone had left the lights on and now there was a dead battery. It didn't take long to enliven it with jumper cables. At one o'clock in the morning they drove to the cottages where they had stayed previously. They pulled the drapes shut so it was dark for some serious sleeping. The cottage brought back fresh memories to Glen because it was across the drive from where we had stayed during our tractor trip.

Sunday morning the Ohioans attended church in Fairbanks with some of the radio staff.

Duane and John visited with staff personnel on Monday afternoon and ate with them while Glen was a guest of Tim and Debb Beck at a Chinese restaurant. The Becks had given us their pickup truck to use last summer while we were in North Pole. A kind gesture like that was so much appreciated and reminded us to be generous to others.

It seemed like the men had an extra day since they left the reservation earlier than planned when the residents went to Tok to celebrate. They decided to make it a pleasure day and went on a bus tour of Denali State Park.

Time for departure came and they rode the shuttle bus from Fairbanks to Anchorage. Now they were very eager to get to the airport and head for Phoenix, Arizona and then on to Columbus, Ohio. It wasn't worthwhile going to a motel since the schedule called for a 1:30 AM departure.

They decided they could hang around in the airport to kill time. Shortly before the time to board the plane, an announcement over the public address system informed them the flight would be delayed three hours because of a dust storm in Phoenix. Also, they said the Phoenix Airport was closed because President Clinton was there.

What a letdown! They were extremely tired and now what should they do for another three hours? Glen found a spot to lie down on the floor by the wall where no one would step on him. He used his carry-on bag for a pillow and slept awhile until the air-conditioning made him too cool. Sure wasn't like the comfort of home!

About 50 feet away, Duane found a spot to sleep on the floor. The air-conditioning kept him from sleeping very long, too.

John tried to sleep while sitting up, but couldn't, so he walked around and stayed out of trouble. The night security guard asked John if he knew the two men sleeping on the floor. John explained the situation. The guard probably thought Glen and Duane were homeless men seeking shelter. It must have been quite a sight.

Three weary men finally boarded the plane for an uneventful ride to Phoenix where it was over 100°. The last leg of the trip was to Columbus, Ohio, where their wives and some family members greeted them. Pastor Larry Hasemeyer had taken some of the people to Columbus in the church van so they could visit with the travelers during the ride home.

We returned to our homes with grateful hearts, knowing that God's will was done and anticipating His guidance for the future.